TT
778
.C76
L45
1995

W9-BSP-991

# LEISURE ARTS' BEST
# 250
# Christmas Quickies

LEISURE ARTS, INC.
and
OXMOOR HOUSE, INC.

## EDITORIAL STAFF

**Vice President and Editor-in-Chief:**
Anne Van Wagner Childs
**Executive Director:** Sandra Graham Case
**Executive Editor:** Susan Frantz Wiles
**Publications Director:** Carla Bentley
**Creative Art Director:** Gloria Bearden
**Production Art Director:** Melinda Stout

### EDITORIAL
**Associate Editor:** Linda L. Trimble
**Senior Editorial Writer:** Laura Lee Weland
**Editorial Associates:** Robyn Sheffield-Edwards,
Tammi Williamson Bradley, and Terri Leming Davidson

### TECHNICAL
**Managing Editor:** Lisa Truxton Curton
**Senior Technical Writer:** Donna Brown Hill

### FOODS
**Foods Editor:** Celia Fahr Harkey, R.D.
**Assistant Foods Editor:** Jane Kenner Prather
**Test Kitchen Assistants:** Nora Faye Spencer Clift and
Leslie Belote Dunn

### ART
**Book/Magazine Art Director:** Diane M. Ghegan
**Senior Production Artist:** Leslie Loring Krebs

## BUSINESS STAFF

**Publisher:** Bruce Akin
**Vice President, Finance:** Tom Siebenmorgen
**Vice President, Retail Sales:** Thomas L. Carlisle
**Retail Sales Director:** Richard Tignor
**Vice President, Retail Marketing:** Pam Stebbins
**Retail Customer Services Director:** Margaret Sweetin

**Marketing Manager:** Russ Barnett
**Executive Director of Marketing and Circulation:**
Guy A. Crossley
**Circulation Manager:** Byron L. Taylor
**Print Production Manager:** Laura Lockhart
**Print Production Coordinator:** Nancy Reddick Lister

Library of Congress Catalog Number 95-75506
Hardcover ISBN 0-942237-75-7
Softcover ISBN 0-942237-76-5

# Introduction

*As the hustle and bustle of the Christmas season rolls around, people often find themselves running out of time to prepare for the holidays. With this in mind, we developed this fabulous treasury of Yuletide cross stitch projects. They're all designed to be finished quickly, leaving you free to focus on other important things — like cooking Christmas dinner! With designs spanning nearly 10 years of Leisure Arts publications, 250 Christmas Quickies offers something for everyone. You'll find homemade gifts for friends and family, Christmas tree ornaments, festive clothing items, and projects to decorate your home for the holiday season. So from our house to yours, may your holidays be the best ever!*

# Table

# of Contents

# Quick-as-a-Wink Ornaments

Trimming the Christmas tree is a beloved custom that brings enjoyment to people of all ages. To make the tradition even more special, treasured ornaments are often passed down from one generation to another as symbols of love and unity. Now you can create your own holiday heirlooms by making any of the tree-trimmers in this collection. Whether you're stitching for your own tree or making decorations to share with family members or friends, these designs will be delightful for one and all.

# A Festive Medley

*This medley of merry motifs will add a jolly touch to the Yuletide season. We created ornaments by framing the entire collection in mini wreaths. For another exciting project, try stitching these festive little designs on a keepsake afghan (shown on the next page).*

# Versatile Holiday Motifs

*These tiny Yuletide motifs add a cute touch to this afghan for the holidays, and they'll give any project a fun look. You can stitch them on party favors, guest towels, mini pillows, and much more. Whatever they adorn, these versatile designs will deliver lots of Christmas charm!*

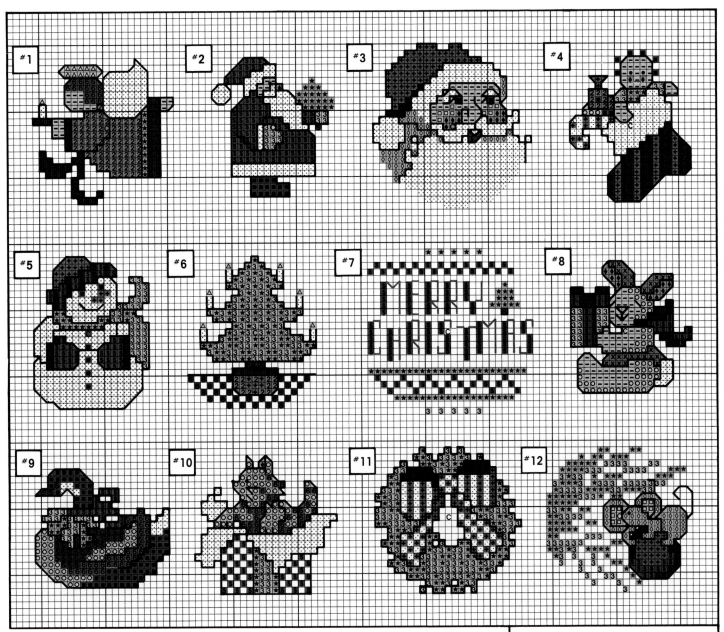

**Mini Wreaths:** Designs (shown on pages 6 and 7) stitched on 7" squares of Antique White Aida (18 ct). Two strands of floss used for Cross Stitch and 1 for all other stitches. Made into ornaments (see Mini Wreaths Finishing, page 143).

**Afghan:** Seven of the designs stitched over 2 fabric threads on a 1¼ yd piece of Soft White Anne Cloth (18 ct). Six strands of floss used for Cross Stitch and 2 for all other stitches. See Afghan Finishing, page 143, to fringe afghan. Refer to Diagram for placement of designs on fabric.

**DIAGRAM**

| 2 | 3 | 5 |
|---|---|---|
|   | 4 | 1 |
| 11 | 2 | 6 |
|   | 5 | 4 |
| 3 | 6 | 11 |
|   | 1 | 5 |
| 2 | 3 | 4 |

| X | DMC | ¼X | B'ST | ANC. | COLOR |
|---|-----|-----|------|------|-------|
| | blanc | | | 02 | white |
| | 300 | | | 0352 | brown |
| 6 | 301 | | | 0349 | rust |
| | 310 | | / | 0403 | black |
| 2 | 312 | | | 0147 | blue |
| 5 | 321 | | / | 047 | red |
| X | 437 | | | 0368 | tan |
| | 498 | | | 020 | dk red |
| + | 666 | | | 046 | lt red |
| ★ | 699 | | | 0923 | dk green |
| 3 | 701 | | | 0227 | green |
| △ | 726 | | | 0297 | yellow |
| ○ | 738 | | | 0367 | lt tan |
| − | 739 | | | 0366 | beige |
| □ | 754 | | | 4146 | flesh |
| ◆ | 761 | | | 08 | pink |
| ◇ | 762 | | | 0397 | grey |
| • | 310 | | black French Knot | | |
| C | Approx. center of design. | | | | |

9

# American Christmas Spirit

*Our inspiration for these mini pillow ornaments came from the
Victorian tradition of displaying allegiance by trimming the tree
with patriotic emblems. These star-spangled treasures are sure
to add spirit to your holiday celebration!*

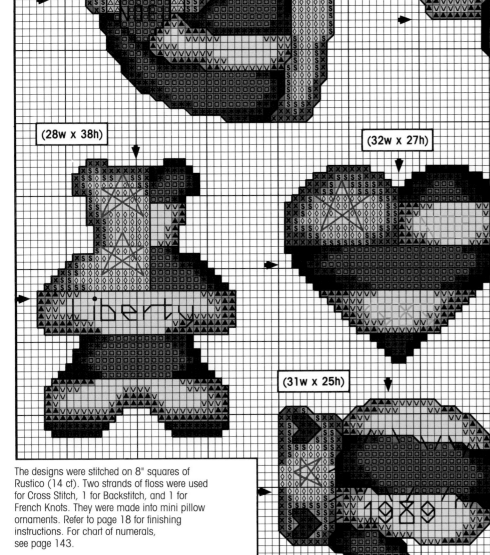

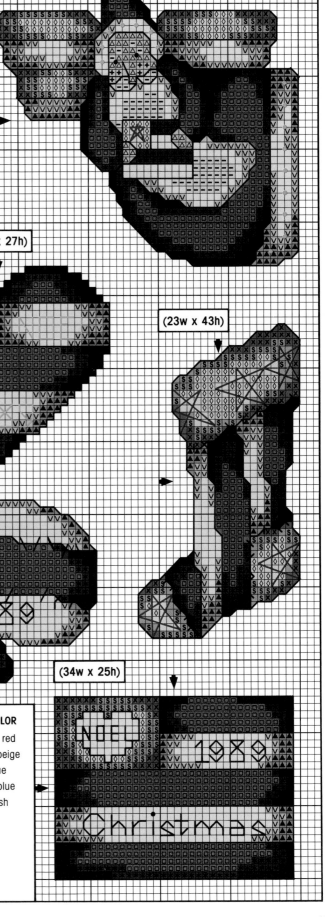

**(42w x 34h)**

**(43w x 40h)**

**(28w x 38h)**

**(32w x 27h)**

**(23w x 43h)**

**(31w x 25h)**

**(34w x 25h)**

Liberty

1989

NOEL 1989

Christmas

The designs were stitched on 8" squares of Rustico (14 ct). Two strands of floss were used for Cross Stitch, 1 for Backstitch, and 1 for French Knots. They were made into mini pillow ornaments. Refer to page 18 for finishing instructions. For chart of numerals, see page 143.

*Designed by Sue McElhaney.*

| X | DMC | ¼X | B'ST | ANC. | COLOR | X | DMC | ¼X | B'ST | ANC. | COLOR |
|---|---|---|---|---|---|---|---|---|---|---|---|
| - | ecru | | /* | 0926 | ecru | | 815 | | | 044 | dk red |
| * | 304 | | | 047 | red | | 822 | | | 0390 | lt beige |
| | 310 | | / | 0403 | black | S | 930 | | | 0922 | blue |
| X | 311 | | / | 0148 | dk blue | ◊ | 931 | | | 0921 | lt blue |
| □ | 321 | | | 013 | lt red | △ | 948 | | | 0892 | flesh |
| ★ | 434 | | | 0310 | brown | ● | ecru | | ecru French Knot | | |
| ▲ | 642 | | | 0392 | dk beige | ● | 310 | | black French Knot | | |
| V | 644 | | | 0391 | beige | ● | 311 | | dk blue French Knot | | |
| O | 676 | | | 0891 | yellow | *Work in long stitches. | | | | | |
| + | 761 | | | 08 | pink | | | | | | |

# Symbols of the Season

*Spread wishes for a joyous Noel with these quick-and-easy ornaments. Reflecting traditional symbols of the season, these pretty tree-trimmers can also be used as stocking stuffers, package tie-ons, or wreath accents.*

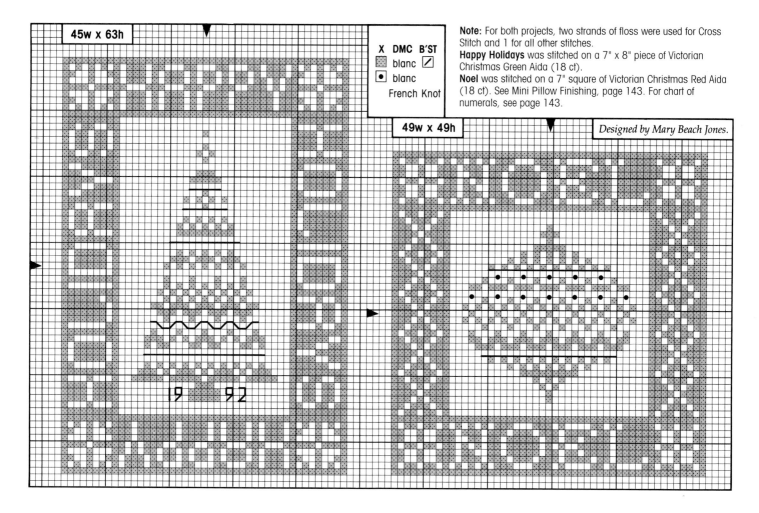

**Note:** For both projects, two strands of floss were used for Cross Stitch and 1 for all other stitches.

**Happy Holidays** was stitched on a 7" x 8" piece of Victorian Christmas Green Aida (18 ct).

**Noel** was stitched on a 7" square of Victorian Christmas Red Aida (18 ct). See Mini Pillow Finishing, page 143. For chart of numerals, see page 143.

Designed by Mary Beach Jones.

| X | DMC | B'ST |
|---|-----|------|
| (shaded) | blanc | / |
| (dot) | blanc | |
| | French Knot | |

45w x 63h

49w x 49h

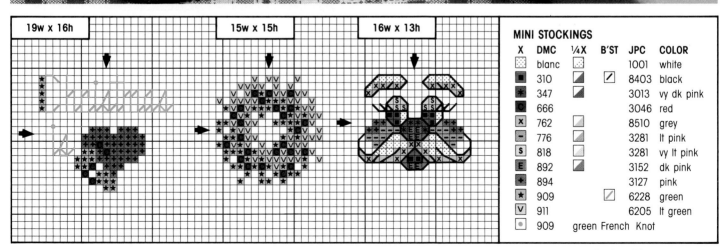

# Merry Mini Stockings

*Accented with one of our simple motifs, these festive mini stockings make merry gifts for anyone on your Christmas list. They can also be used as ornaments or package decorations. The quick-to-stitch projects are especially nice if your time is limited or you're a beginning stitcher.*

**19w x 16h**

**15w x 15h**

**16w x 13h**

## MINI STOCKINGS

| X | DMC | ¼X | B'ST | JPC | COLOR |
|---|-----|-----|------|-----|-------|
| ░ | blanc | ░ | | 1001 | white |
| ■ | 310 | ◪ | ⁄ | 8403 | black |
| ✳ | 347 | ◪ | | 3013 | vy dk pink |
| ◉ | 666 | | | 3046 | red |
| X | 762 | ◪ | | 8510 | grey |
| - | 776 | ◪ | | 3281 | lt pink |
| S | 818 | ◪ | | 3281 | vy lt pink |
| E | 892 | ◪ | | 3152 | dk pink |
| ✦ | 894 | | | 3127 | pink |
| ★ | 909 | | ◪ | 6228 | green |
| V | 911 | | | 6205 | lt green |
| ● | 909 | green French Knot | | | |

Each design stitched on the Aida (14 ct) insert of a mini stocking. Three strands of floss used for Cross Stitch and 1 for all other stitches.

*Designed by Sam Hawkins.*

# Nostalgic Linen Trims

*Stitched on unbleached linen, these delightful ornaments have an antique quality. The naturally aged appearance of the fabric enhances the nostalgic look of these old-fashioned holiday designs.*

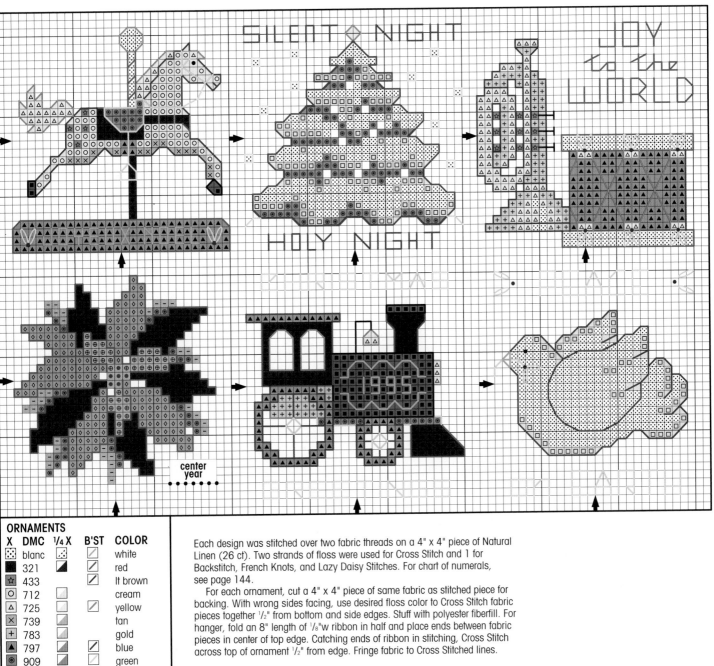

## ORNAMENTS

| X | DMC | ¼ X | B'ST | COLOR |
|---|-----|-----|------|-------|
| ⊡ | blanc | ⊡ | ◪ | white |
| ■ | 321 | ◪ | ◪ | red |
| ☆ | 433 | | ◪ | lt brown |
| ○ | 712 | ◻ | | cream |
| △ | 725 | ◻ | ◪ | yellow |
| × | 739 | ◪ | | tan |
| + | 783 | ◪ | | gold |
| ▲ | 797 | ◪ | ◪ | blue |
| ◉ | 909 | ◪ | ◻ | green |
| − | 912 | | | lt green |
| | 946 | ◪ | ◪ | orange |
| ▢ | 3325 | ◻ | ◪ | lt blue |
| ■ | 3371 | ◪ | ◪ | brown |
| ◇ | 3705 | | | coral |
| ⊕ | 3708 | | | lt coral |
| ● | 321 | | | red French Knot |
| ● | 783 | | | gold French Knot |
| ● | 3371 | | | brown French Knot |
| ◿ | 909 | | | green Lazy Daisy Stitch |

Each design was stitched over two fabric threads on a 4" x 4" piece of Natural Linen (26 ct). Two strands of floss were used for Cross Stitch and 1 for Backstitch, French Knots, and Lazy Daisy Stitches. For chart of numerals, see page 144.

For each ornament, cut a 4" x 4" piece of same fabric as stitched piece for backing. With wrong sides facing, use desired floss color to Cross Stitch fabric pieces together ½" from bottom and side edges. Stuff with polyester fiberfill. For hanger, fold an 8" length of ⅛"w ribbon in half and place ends between fabric pieces in center of top edge. Catching ends of ribbon in stitching, Cross Stitch across top of ornament ½" from edge. Fringe fabric to Cross Stitched lines.

*Designs by Terrie Lee Steinmeyer.*

### ORNAMENTS (approx 28w x 28h)

| | |
|---|---|
| Aida 11 | 2⅝" x 2⅝" |
| Aida 14 | 2" x 2" |
| Aida 18 | 1⅝" x 1⅝" |
| Hardanger 22 | 1⅜" x 1⅜" |

# Gift Ornaments

*For those important presents that require extra-special wrapping, add one of these gift ornaments. Later, they can be used as Christmas tree decorations, and your little gifts will keep on giving, year after year.*

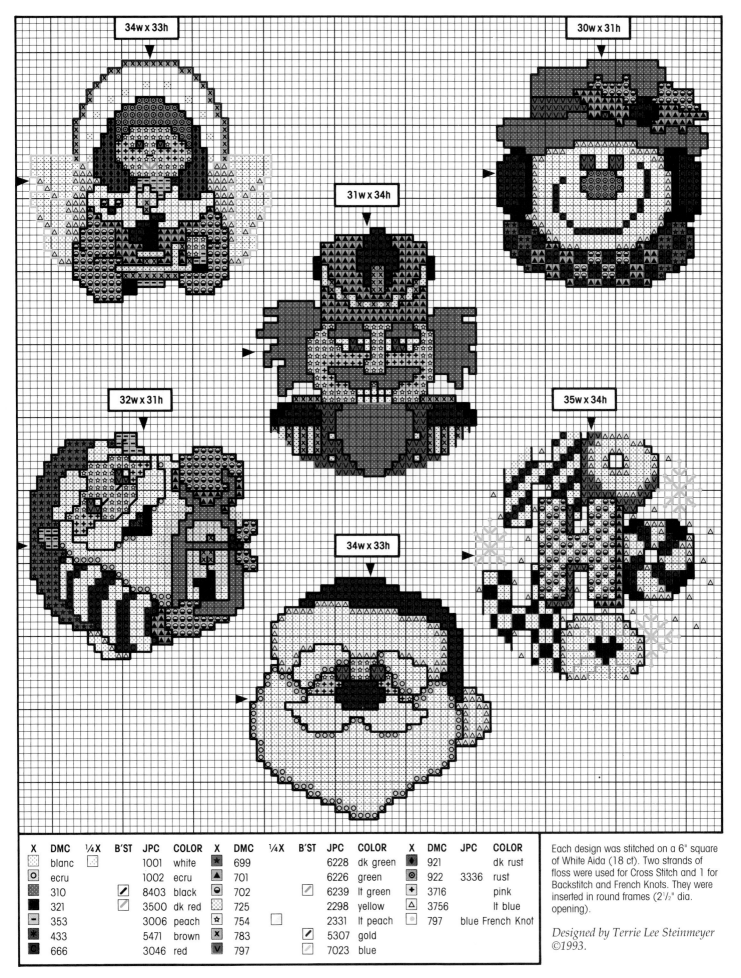

34w x 33h

30w x 31h

31w x 34h

32w x 31h

35w x 34h

34w x 33h

| X | DMC | 1/4 X | B'ST | JPC | COLOR | X | DMC | 1/4 X | B'ST | JPC | COLOR | X | DMC | JPC | COLOR |
|---|-----|-------|------|-----|-------|---|-----|-------|------|-----|-------|---|-----|-----|-------|
| | blanc | | | 1001 | white | ★ | 699 | | | 6228 | dk green | ◆ | 921 | | dk rust |
| ◎ | ecru | | | 1002 | ecru | ▲ | 701 | | | 6226 | green | ◎ | 922 | 3336 | rust |
| | 310 | | ✎ | 8403 | black | ◉ | 702 | | ✎ | 6239 | lt green | ✛ | 3716 | | pink |
| ■ | 321 | | ✎ | 3500 | dk red | | 725 | | | 2298 | yellow | △ | 3756 | | lt blue |
| ▬ | 353 | | | 3006 | peach | ★ | 754 | | | 2331 | lt peach | ◎ | 797 | | blue French Knot |
| ✳ | 433 | | | 5471 | brown | ✕ | 783 | | ✎ | 5307 | gold | | | | |
| ◨ | 666 | | | 3046 | red | ▼ | 797 | | ✎ | 7023 | blue | | | | |

Each design was stitched on a 6" square of White Aida (18 ct). Two strands of floss were used for Cross Stitch and 1 for Backstitch and French Knots. They were inserted in round frames (2½" dia. opening).

*Designed by Terrie Lee Steinmeyer ©1993.*

# Santa's Helpers

*Dressed in holiday suits and hugging candy canes, this winsome elf and his pudgy bear companion eagerly await Santa's arrival. Whether you use these mini pillows as basket accents, gift tags, or ornaments for the tree, they're sure to bring joy to all who see them.*

The designs were stitched on 5" squares of Ivory Aida (14 ct). Three strands of floss were used for Cross Stitch, 1 for Backstitch, and 1 for French Knots. They were made into fringed mini pillows.

For each mini pillow, cut stitched piece 1" larger than design on all sides. Use a piece of same fabric as stitched piece for backing; cut fabric the same size as stitched piece. With wrong sides facing, use desired floss color to cross stitch fabric pieces together ½" from sides and bottom edge. Stuff with polyester fiberfill. Cross stitch across top of pillow ½" from edge. Fringe fabric to cross-stitched lines. For hanging pillow, attach ribbon to top center back of mini pillow. For pillow on basket, attach mini pillow to side of market basket with craft glue.

*Designed by Marianne Wourms.*

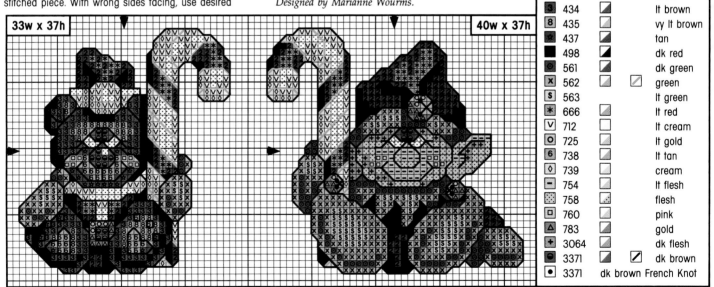

| X | DMC | ¼X | B'ST | COLOR |
|---|---|---|---|---|
| ▨ | blanc | ▨ | | white |
| 2 | 321 | ◪ | ◪ | red |
| ■ | 433 | ◪ | | brown |
| 3 | 434 | ◪ | | lt brown |
| 8 | 435 | ◪ | | vy lt brown |
| ★ | 437 | ◪ | | tan |
| ■ | 498 | ◪ | | dk red |
| ◉ | 561 | ◪ | | dk green |
| X | 562 | ◪ | ◪ | green |
| S | 563 | | | lt green |
| * | 666 | ◪ | | lt red |
| V | 712 | ☐ | | lt cream |
| O | 725 | ◪ | | lt gold |
| 6 | 738 | ◪ | | lt tan |
| ◇ | 739 | ◪ | | cream |
| - | 754 | ◪ | | lt flesh |
| ▨ | 758 | ▨ | | flesh |
| ▢ | 760 | ◪ | | pink |
| △ | 783 | ◪ | | gold |
| ✛ | 3064 | ◪ | | dk flesh |
| ◨ | 3371 | ◪ | ◪ | dk brown |
| • | 3371 | | | dk brown French Knot |

**33w x 37h**      **40w x 37h**

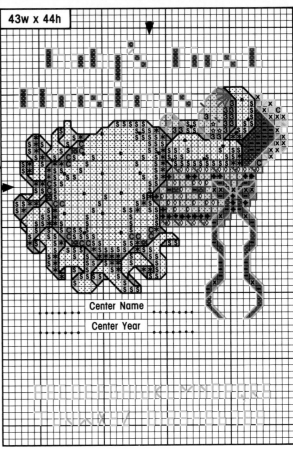

# Baby's First Christmas

*A special way to commemorate a little one's first Christmas, this sweet mini pillow is personalized with baby's name and the year. The ornament will make a wonderful keepsake!*

**43w x 44h**

| X | DMC | ¼X | B'ST | ANC. | COLOR | X | DMC | ¼X | B'ST | ANC. | COLOR |
|---|-----|----|------|------|-------|---|-----|----|------|------|-------|
| | blanc | | | 2 | white | | 758 | | | 882 | dk peach |
| | 334 | | | 977 | dk blue | | 760 | | | 1022 | pink |
| | 347 | | | 1025 | dk rose | | 761 | | | 1021 | lt pink |
| 3 | 353 | | | 6 | peach | | 775 | | | 128 | lt blue |
| C | 367 | | | 217 | green | | 801 | | | 359 | brown |
| X | 368 | | | 214 | lt green | | 948 | | | 1011 | lt peach |
| | 676 | | | 891 | gold | | 3325 | | | 129 | blue |
| | 677 | | | 886 | lt gold | | 3328 | | | 1024 | rose |
| | 729 | | | 890 | dk gold | | 3328 | | | | rose French Knot |

**Ornament:** Stitched over 2 fabric threads on a 9" square of Antique White Belfast Linen (32 ct). Two strands of floss used for Cross Stitch and 1 for Backstitch and French Knots. To personalize, stitch name and year using DMC 347 floss and alphabet and numbers provided. Made into an ornament.

**For ornament, you will need** an approx. 4½" square of linen for back, an approx. 4½" square of fabric for lining, 18" length of ¼" dia. twisted satin cord, polyester fiberfill, thread, and hand sewing needle.
**(Note:** Use ¼" seam allowance for all seams.)
For ornament front, trim stitched piece approx. ¾" from design on all sides. Trim backing fabric and lining fabric to same size as stitched piece. Matching raw edges and right side of lining fabric to wrong side of stitched piece, baste lining fabric and stitched piece together close to raw edges. Matching right sides, raw edges, and leaving an opening for turning, sew ornament front and back together. Trim corners diagonally and turn ornament right side out. Stuff ornament with polyester fiberfill and sew final closure by hand. Hand-sew satin cord around edges of pillow, overlapping ends.

*Design by Lorri Birmingham.*

Center Name

Center Year

# Fancy Little Stockings

*Shimmering glass seed beads spell Christmas greetings on this trio of fancy little linen stockings. For a special touch, fill the stockings with cinnamon sticks, greenery, or tiny gifts.*

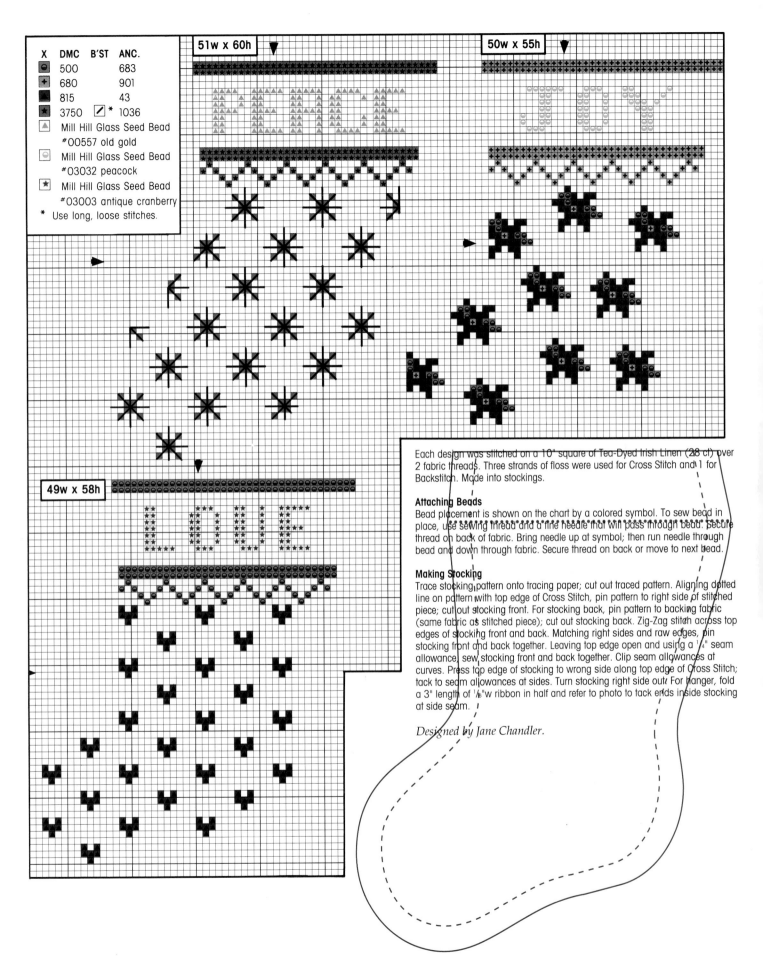

| X | DMC | B'ST | ANC. |
|---|-----|------|------|
| ⊖ | 500 | | 683 |
| + | 680 | | 901 |
| ◼ | 815 | | 43 |
| ★ | 3750 | ⁄ * | 1036 |
| ▲ | Mill Hill Glass Seed Bead #00557 old gold | | |
| ⊙ | Mill Hill Glass Seed Bead #03032 peacock | | |
| ★ | Mill Hill Glass Seed Bead #03003 antique cranberry | | |
| * | Use long, loose stitches. | | |

**51w x 60h**

**50w x 55h**

**49w x 58h**

Each design was stitched on a 10" square of Tea-Dyed Irish Linen (28 ct) over 2 fabric threads. Three strands of floss were used for Cross Stitch and 1 for Backstitch. Made into stockings.

**Attaching Beads**

Bead placement is shown on the chart by a colored symbol. To sew bead in place, use sewing thread and a fine needle that will pass through bead. Secure thread on back of fabric. Bring needle up at symbol; then run needle through bead and down through fabric. Secure thread on back or move to next bead.

**Making Stocking**

Trace stocking pattern onto tracing paper; cut out traced pattern. Aligning dotted line on pattern with top edge of Cross Stitch, pin pattern to right side of stitched piece; cut out stocking front. For stocking back, pin pattern to backing fabric (same fabric as stitched piece); cut out stocking back. Zig-Zag stitch across top edges of stocking front and back. Matching right sides and raw edges, pin stocking front and back together. Leaving top edge open and using a ¼" seam allowance, sew stocking front and back together. Clip seam allowances at curves. Press top edge of stocking to wrong side along top edge of Cross Stitch; tack to seam allowances at sides. Turn stocking right side out. For hanger, fold a 3" length of ⅛"w ribbon in half and refer to photo to tack ends inside stocking at side seam.

*Designed by Jane Chandler.*

# Button Love

*These sweet fringed mini pillows make cute tree-trimmers, package ties, or even basket embellishments. They're quick and easy to create by simply adding a ceramic button featuring your favorite holiday character below the cross-stitched phrase.*

The design was stitched on an 8" x 7" piece of Dirty Aida (14 ct). Center design horizontally with top of design 2½" from top of fabric piece. Three strands of floss were used for Cross Stitch. Refer to photo for button placement and hand sew button in place.

For each mini pillow, trim stitched piece 1" larger than design (including button) on all sides. Use a piece of same fabric as stitched piece for backing; cut fabric the same size as stitched piece. With wrong sides facing, use 2 strands of red floss and Running Stitches (**Fig. 1**) to join fabric pieces together ½" from bottom and side edges. Stuff with polyester fiberfill. Repeat to stitch across top of mini pillow ½" from edge. Fringe fabric to within one square of stitched lines.

## STITCH DIAGRAM

**Running Stitch:** Work Running Stitch as shown in **Fig. 1**, stitching over and under 1 fabric thread.

**Fig. 1**

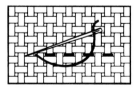

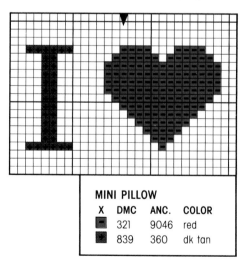

**MINI PILLOW**

| X | DMC | ANC. | COLOR |
|---|-----|------|-------|
| ■ | 321 | 9046 | red |
| ✕ | 839 | 360 | dk tan |

# Delightful Dozen

*This charming set of ornaments offers something for everyone! The twelve classic designs, which include Santa Claus, candy canes, angels, and more, are sure to occupy a special place in your heart — and on your tree!*

The designs (shown on page 23) were each stitched on a 6" square of Antique White Aida (18 ct). Two strands of floss were used for Cross Stitch and 1 for Backstitch (work dk yellow Backstitch in long stitches), and French Knots. They were inserted in purchased round frames (2½" dia. opening).

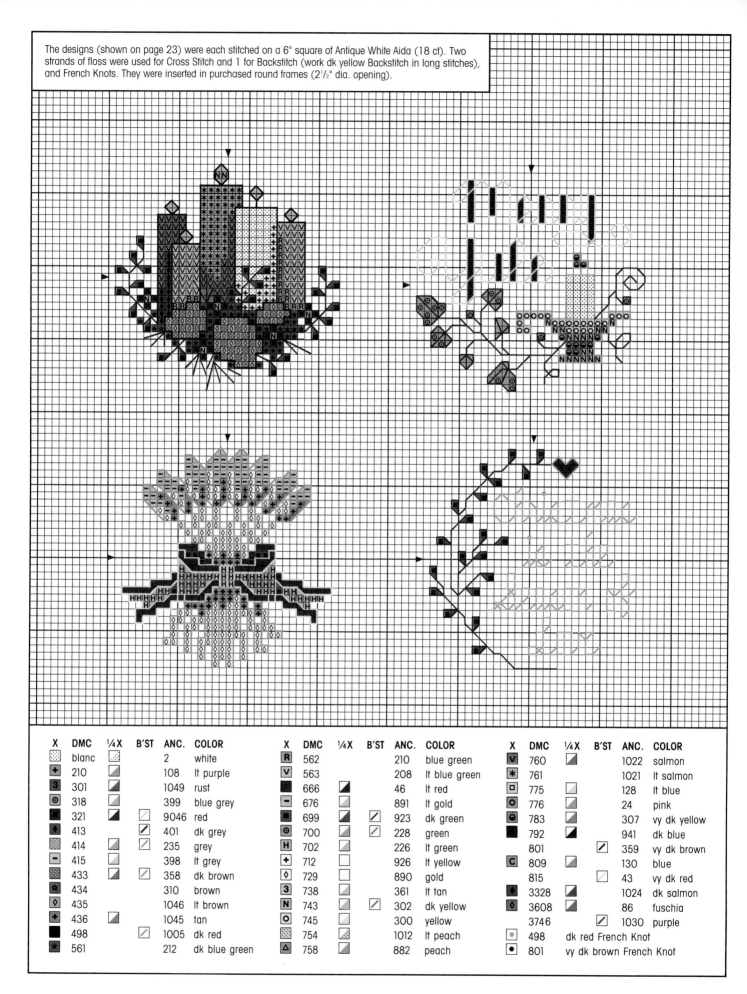

| X | DMC | ¼X | B'ST | ANC. | COLOR | X | DMC | ¼X | B'ST | ANC. | COLOR | X | DMC | ¼X | B'ST | ANC. | COLOR |
|---|-----|-----|------|------|-------|---|-----|-----|------|------|-------|---|-----|-----|------|------|-------|
| | blanc | | | 2 | white | R | 562 | | | 210 | blue green | V | 760 | | | 1022 | salmon |
| + | 210 | | | 108 | lt purple | V | 563 | | | 208 | lt blue green | * | 761 | | | 1021 | lt salmon |
| 3 | 301 | | | 1049 | rust | | 666 | | | 46 | lt red | □ | 775 | | | 128 | lt blue |
| ⊙ | 318 | | | 399 | blue grey | − | 676 | | | 891 | lt gold | O | 776 | | | 24 | pink |
| ■ | 321 | | | 9046 | red | ■ | 699 | | | 923 | dk green | ◐ | 783 | | | 307 | vy dk yellow |
| ◆ | 413 | | | 401 | dk grey | ⊙ | 700 | | | 228 | green | ■ | 792 | | | 941 | dk blue |
| | 414 | | | 235 | grey | H | 702 | | | 226 | lt green | | 801 | | | 359 | vy dk brown |
| − | 415 | | | 398 | lt grey | + | 712 | | | 926 | lt yellow | C | 809 | | | 130 | blue |
| ◈ | 433 | | | 358 | dk brown | ◊ | 729 | | | 890 | gold | | 815 | | | 43 | vy dk red |
| ✦ | 434 | | | 310 | brown | 3 | 738 | | | 361 | lt tan | ◆ | 3328 | | | 1024 | dk salmon |
| ◇ | 435 | | | 1046 | lt brown | N | 743 | | | 302 | dk yellow | ◇ | 3608 | | | 86 | fuschia |
| + | 436 | | | 1045 | tan | O | 745 | | | 300 | yellow | | 3746 | | | 1030 | purple |
| ■ | 498 | | | 1005 | dk red | ▦ | 754 | | | 1012 | lt peach | ⊙ | 498 | | | | dk red French Knot |
| ★ | 561 | | | 212 | dk blue green | △ | 758 | | | 882 | peach | ● | 801 | | | | vy dk brown French Knot |

# Yuletide Messages

*To create our cheerful Christmas ornaments, we stiffened the fabric so the designs could be cut out without fraying. You'll want to stitch them all to fill your tree with warm Yuletide messages.*

(40w x 21h)

Goodwill Toward Men

(39w x 19h)

Let the Land Rejoice

(40w x 23h)

Peace to all on Christmas

(36w x 25h)

Christmas is a time for Sharing

(31w x 34h)

Christmas is Love

(22w x 33h)

Good Tidings To All

(34w x 21h)

Good Cheer

(37w x 17h)

Welcome the Peace of Christmas

| X | DMC | ¼X | B'ST | ANC. | COLOR |
|---|-----|-----|------|------|-------|
| | blanc | | | 02 | white |
| | 310 | | ✓ | 0403 | black |
| | 321 | | | 047 | red |
| | 433 | | | 0371 | brown |
| | 434 | | | 0310 | lt brown |
| | 666 | | | 046 | lt red |
| | 699 | | ✓ | 0229 | green |
| | 701 | | | 0227 | lt green |
| | 725 | | | 0306 | lt gold |
| | 754 | | | 4146 | flesh |
| | 783 | | | 0307 | gold |
| | 797 | | | 0132 | lt blue |
| | 820 | | | 0134 | blue |
| | 310 | | | | black French Knot |
| | 666 | | | | lt red French Knot |

Each design was stitched on a 5" square piece of Ivory Aida (14 ct). Two strands of floss were used for Cross Stitch and 1 for Backstitch and French Knots. They were made into ornaments.

For each ornament, cut a piece of cotton fabric for backing same size as stitched piece. Apply fabric stiffener to back of stitched piece. Place backing fabric on stitched piece and allow to dry. Apply stiffener to back of design and allow to dry. Trim to 1 square from edges of design. To prevent fraying, apply a small amount of fabric glue to edges of design and allow to dry.

For hanger, thread a length of nylon line through top center of ornament and knot ends.

# Christmas Patches

*To add a country look to your Christmas tree, stitch up these four fringed mini pillows! With designs including a wreath, Santa, a stocking, and an angel, they'll soon become Yuletide favorites.*

| X | DMC | ¼X | B'ST | JPC | COLOR | | X | DMC | ¼X | B'ST | JPC | COLOR |
|---|---|---|---|---|---|---|---|---|---|---|---|---|
| - | ecru | ☐ | | 1002 | ecru | | ◇ | 783 | | ◪ | 5307 | lt gold |
| | 310 | | ◪ | 8403 | black | | ■ | 814 | | ◪ | 3044 | dk red |
| ◇ | 312 | | | 7979 | lt blue | | ▨ | 815 | | | 3000 | red |
| ◎ | 319 | ◪ | ◪ | 6246 | dk green | | ✕ | 822 | | ◪ | 5830 | lt beige grey |
| ▲ | 336 | | ◪ | 7981 | dk blue | | ▨ | 839 | | | 5360 | dk beige brown |
| ▣ | 347 | | | 3013 | dk salmon | | ◆ | 840 | | | 5379 | beige brown |
| | 356 | | ◪ | 2338 | dk flesh | | ◎ | 841 | | | 5376 | lt beige brown |
| ★ | 367 | | | 6018 | green | | ◎ | 926 | | ◪ | 6007 | grey blue |
| ◆ | 434 | | | 5000 | brown | | ☆ | 927 | | ◪ | 6006 | lt grey blue |
| V | 435 | | | 5371 | lt brown | | ✚ | 3033 | | | 5388 | vy lt beige brown |
| | 610 | | ◪ | 5889 | dk khaki | | ◆ | 3328 | | | 3071 | salmon |
| 4 | 612 | | | | lt khaki | | ■ | 3345 | | | 6258 | dk yellow green |
| 2 | 613 | | | | vy lt khaki | | ✳ | 3346 | | | 6258 | yellow green |
| △ | 644 | | | 5831 | beige grey | | ▢ | 3779 | | ◪ | | lt flesh |
| ○ | 725 | ☐ | | 2298 | yellow | | • | 310 | | | 8403 | black Fr. Knot |
| ▨ | 760 | ◪ | | 3069 | vy lt salmon | | • | 815 | | | 3000 | red Fr. Knot |
| | 781 | | ◪ | 5309 | dk gold | | • | 822 | | | 5830 | lt beige grey Fr. Knot |
| ✳ | 782 | | | 5308 | gold | | | | | | | |

STOCKING (43w x 43h)
SANTA (41w x 41h)
WREATH (41w x 41h)
ANGEL (41w x 41h)

Each design was stitched on a 10" square piece of Cream Lugana (25 ct) over two fabric threads using 3 strands of floss for Cross Stitch and 1 strand for Backstitch and French Knots. See Ornament Finishing, pg. 143.

*Designed by Sandi Gore Evans.*

# Tiny Stockings

*These stockings may be tiny, but each is imbued with a generous supply of old-fashioned holiday cheer. Stuffed with Christmas greenery, candy, or a little treasure, they make great decorations for the tree or a special package.*

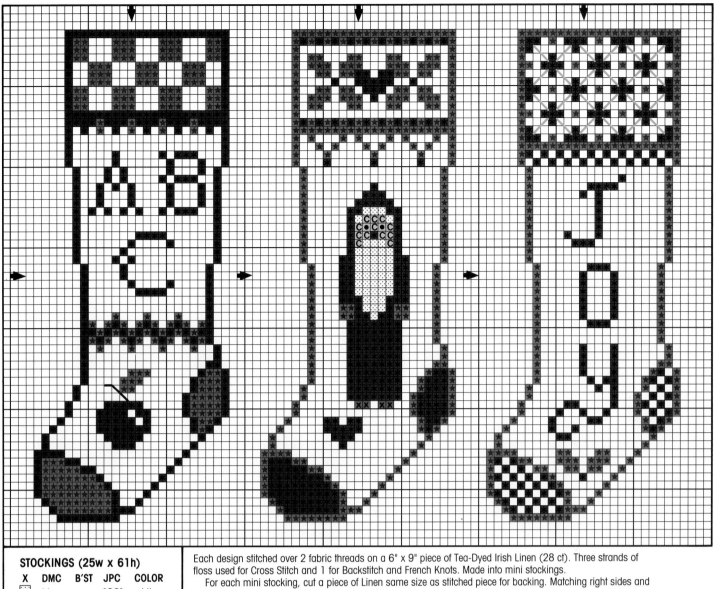

**STOCKINGS (25w x 61h)**

| X | DMC | B'ST | JPC | COLOR |
|---|---|---|---|---|
| ▦ | blanc | | 1001 | white |
| ■ | 498 | | 3410 | red |
| ★ | 895 | ◪ | 6021 | green |
| C | 3773 | | | flesh |
| ✖ | 3781 | ◪ | | brown |
| ● | 3781 | | | brown French Knot |

Each design stitched over 2 fabric threads on a 6" x 9" piece of Tea-Dyed Irish Linen (28 ct). Three strands of floss used for Cross Stitch and 1 for Backstitch and French Knots. Made into mini stockings.

For each mini stocking, cut a piece of Linen same size as stitched piece for backing. Matching right sides and raw edges and leaving top edge open, sew stitched piece and backing fabric together ¼" from design. Trim top edge ½" from design. Trim remaining edges leaving a ¼" seam allowance. Clip curves and turn right side out. Fold and press top edge ¼" to wrong side.

For hanger, cut a 10" length of 2-ply jute. Fold jute in half and tie in an overhand knot approx. 1½" from folded end. Referring to photo, tack hanger to mini stocking; stuff with sprigs of artificial greenery, bay leaves, and cinnamon sticks.

*Designed by Mary Scott.*

# Heirloom Ornaments

*Timeless symbols of Christmas, angels and stars have long been favorite holiday decorations. The tranquil colors and linen fabric used for these mini pillow ornaments give them a lovely heirloom quality. They'll be heavenly on your tree — and also on your packages, wreaths, and other trimmings.*

| X | DMC | ANC. | COLOR |
|---|---|---|---|
| O | 315 | 0970 | mauve |
| ▲ | 844 | 0401 | grey |
| X | 924 | 0851 | blue |
| S | 927 | 0849 | lt blue |
| 6 | 3024 | 0397 | beige |

**STAR (26w x 26h)**

| | | |
|---|---|---|
| Aida 11 | 2½" | x 2½" |
| Aida 14 | 1⅞" | x 1⅞" |
| Aida 18 | 1½" | x 1½" |
| Hardanger 22 | 1¼" | x 1¼" |

**ANGEL (41w x 35h)**

| | | |
|---|---|---|
| Aida 11 | 3¾" | x 3¼" |
| Aida 14 | 3" | x 2½" |
| Aida 18 | 2⅜" | x 2" |
| Hardanger 22 | 1⅞" | x 1⅝" |

**ANGEL WITH HORN (47w x 27h)**

| | | |
|---|---|---|
| Aida 11 | 4⅜" | x 2½" |
| Aida 14 | 3⅜" | x 2" |
| Aida 18 | 2⅝" | x 1½" |
| Hardanger 22 | 2¼" | x 1¼" |

**Mini Pillow Ornaments** were stitched on 7" squares of Raw Belfast Linen (32 ct). The designs were stitched over 2 fabric threads. Two strands of floss were used for Cross Stitch. For chart of numerals, see page 143. They were made into mini pillow ornaments.

For each ornament, cut stitched piece ¾" larger than design on all sides. Cut a piece of cotton fabric same size as stitched piece for backing.

With right sides facing and matching raw edges, use a ¼" seam allowance to sew stitched piece and backing fabric together, leaving an opening at center of top edge. Clip seam allowances at corners. Turn right side out, carefully pushing corners outward. Fold edges of opening ¼" to inside; press. Stuff ornament with polyester fiberfill.

For hanger, fold a 7" length of braided jute in half and insert ½" of each end of braid inside ornament opening; whipstitch opening closed.

*Designed by Kandace Thomas.*

# 12 Days in Miniature

*Bring to mind a familiar carol with these little jewels!
Perfect decorations for a tabletop tree, the cute ornaments
will help you celebrate the twelve days of Christmas.*

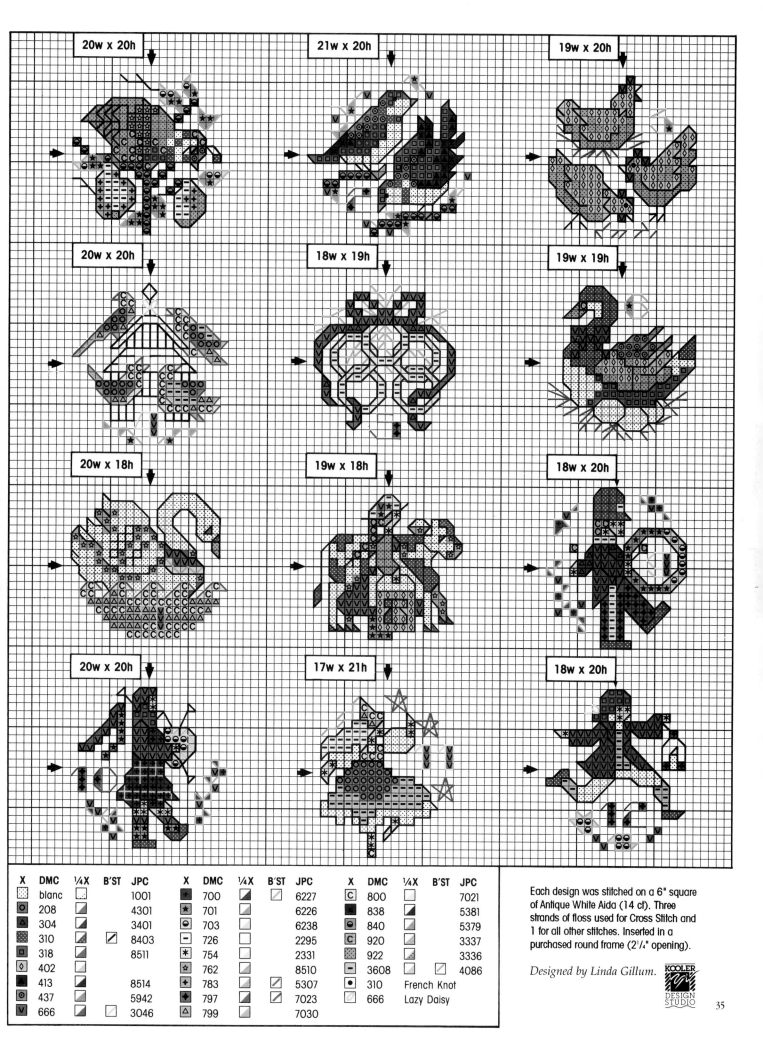

| 20w x 20h | 21w x 20h | 19w x 20h |
| 20w x 20h | 18w x 19h | 19w x 19h |
| 20w x 18h | 19w x 18h | 18w x 20h |
| 20w x 20h | 17w x 21h | 18w x 20h |

| X | DMC | ¼X | B'ST | JPC | X | DMC | ¼X | B'ST | JPC | X | DMC | ¼X | B'ST | JPC |
|---|---|---|---|---|---|---|---|---|---|---|---|---|---|---|
|  | blanc |  |  | 1001 |  | 700 |  |  | 6227 | C | 800 |  |  | 7021 |
|  | 208 |  |  | 4301 |  | 701 |  |  | 6226 |  | 838 |  |  | 5381 |
|  | 304 |  |  | 3401 |  | 703 |  |  | 6238 |  | 840 |  |  | 5379 |
|  | 310 |  |  | 8403 |  | 726 |  |  | 2295 | C | 920 |  |  | 3337 |
|  | 318 |  |  | 8511 |  | 754 |  |  | 2331 |  | 922 |  |  | 3336 |
|  | 402 |  |  |  |  | 762 |  |  | 8510 |  | 3608 |  |  | 4086 |
|  | 413 |  |  |  |  | 783 |  |  | 5307 | • | 310 |  | French Knot |  |
|  | 437 |  |  | 8514 / 5942 |  | 797 |  |  | 7023 |  | 666 |  | Lazy Daisy |  |
|  | 666 |  |  | 3046 |  | 799 |  |  | 7030 |  |  |  |  |  |

Each design was stitched on a 6" square of Antique White Aida (14 ct). Three strands of floss used for Cross Stitch and 1 for all other stitches. Inserted in a purchased round frame (2¼" opening).

*Designed by Linda Gillum.*

KOOLER DESIGN STUDIO

35

# Christmas Story Ornaments

*You'll want to reserve a special place on your tree for these old-fashioned sampler ornaments. Featuring simple motifs and inspirational phrases, they're sure to become holiday keepsakes.*

good tidings of great joy

we have seen his star

the glory of the Lord

peace on earth goodwill toward men

**33w x 78h**

**35w x 46h**

**33w x 77h**

**35w x 46h**

Each design was stitched over 2 fabric threads on an 8" x 13" piece of Tea-Dyed Irish Linen (28 ct). Three strands of floss used for Cross Stitch. Made into ornaments.

For each ornament, trim stitched piece 1" larger than design on all sides. Cut a piece of Irish Linen same size as stitched piece for backing. Matching right sides and raw edges and leaving an opening for turning and stuffing, use a ½" seam allowance to sew stitched piece and backing together. Trim corners diagonally. Turn right side out and use polyester fiberfill to stuff ornament to desired fullness. Whipstitch opening closed.

To make braid, add 5" to outside measurement of ornament and multiply by 3. Cut 2 lengths of six-strand floss the determined measurement. Form two loops by folding floss in half and knot all ends together 1" from ends. Person A holds knotted ends firmly (**Fig. 1**). Counting the number of turns, Person B twists Loop 1 **clockwise** until loop is tight on finger; Person B holds twisted loop tightly in free hand. Twisting the same number of turns, repeat for Loop 2. Person B places both loops on same finger, twists them **counterclockwise** one-half the original number of turns (**Fig. 2**), and knots 1" from end to secure. Beginning and ending at bottom center of ornament, start 1 1/4" from one end of twisted cord and tack twisted cord to edges of ornament, making a loop at top for hanger.

**Fig. 1**  **Fig. 2**

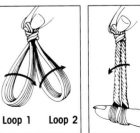

Loop 1  Loop 2

# Hearts for the Holidays

*This heartwarming collection of holiday tree-trimmers offers
a unique way for you to share the spirit of Christmas.
Featuring lots of traditional symbols of the season, the
miniature ornaments will make thoughtful little gifts
for co-workers, teachers, or neighbors.*

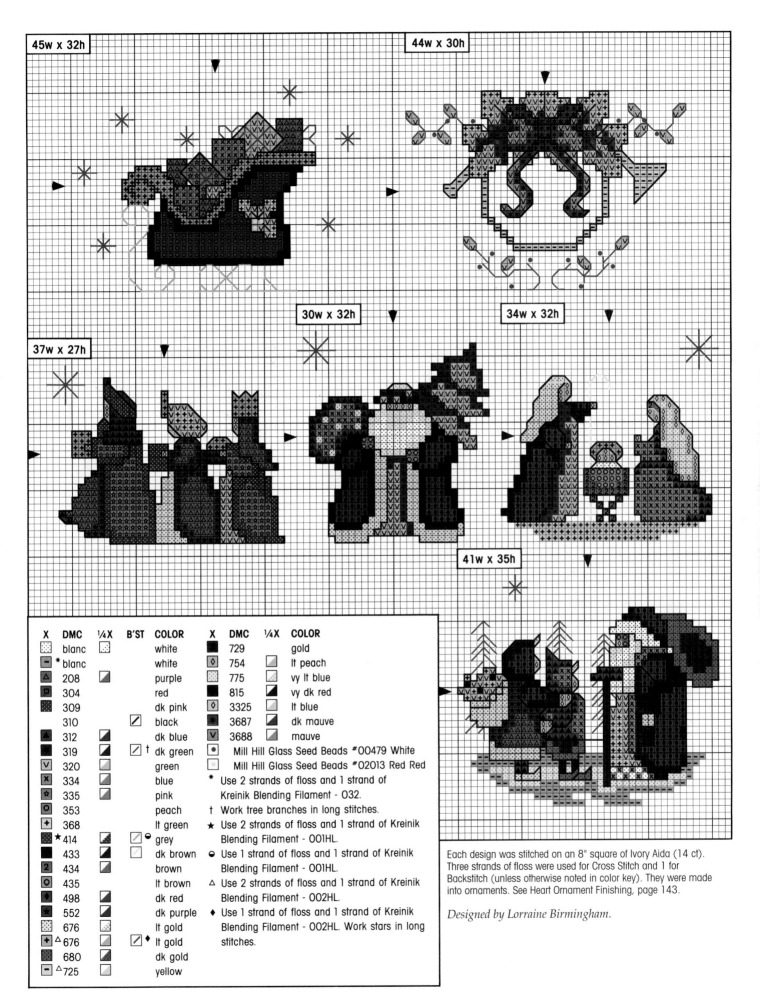

| X | DMC | ¼X | B'ST | COLOR |
|---|---|---|---|---|
| | blanc | | | white |
| − | * blanc | | | white |
| △ | 208 | | | purple |
| | 304 | | | red |
| | 309 | | | dk pink |
| | 310 | | | black |
| | 312 | | | dk blue |
| | 319 | | † | dk green |
| V | 320 | | | green |
| X | 334 | | | blue |
| | 335 | | | pink |
| | 353 | | | peach |
| + | 368 | | | lt green |
| | ★ 414 | | ⊖ | grey |
| | 433 | | | dk brown |
| 2 | 434 | | | brown |
| | 435 | | | lt brown |
| | 498 | | | dk red |
| | 552 | | | dk purple |
| | 676 | | | lt gold |
| + | △ 676 | | ◆ | lt gold |
| | 680 | | | dk gold |
| − | △ 725 | | | yellow |

| X | DMC | ¼X | COLOR |
|---|---|---|---|
| | 729 | | gold |
| ◇ | 754 | | lt peach |
| | 775 | | vy lt blue |
| | 815 | | vy dk red |
| ◇ | 3325 | | lt blue |
| | 3687 | | dk mauve |
| V | 3688 | | mauve |
| ● | Mill Hill Glass Seed Beads #00479 White |
| | Mill Hill Glass Seed Beads #02013 Red Red |

\* Use 2 strands of floss and 1 strand of
Kreinik Blending Filament - O32.

† Work tree branches in long stitches.

★ Use 2 strands of floss and 1 strand of Kreinik
Blending Filament - OO1HL.

⊖ Use 1 strand of floss and 1 strand of Kreinik
Blending Filament - OO1HL.

△ Use 2 strands of floss and 1 strand of Kreinik
Blending Filament - OO2HL.

◆ Use 1 strand of floss and 1 strand of Kreinik
Blending Filament - OO2HL. Work stars in long
stitches.

Each design was stitched on an 8" square of Ivory Aida (14 ct).
Three strands of floss were used for Cross Stitch and 1 for
Backstitch (unless otherwise noted in color key). They were made
into ornaments. See Heart Ornament Finishing, page 143.

*Designed by Lorraine Birmingham.*

# Fast and Festive Fashions

*Getting all dressed up for the Christmas season has never been easier — or quicker — than with the wonderful wearables you'll discover in this collection! There's something for everyone, whether you're looking for a unique holiday outfit for yourself or a family member, or stitching the perfect gift for a friend. The best part about these projects is that each adorable design is small enough to work up in a jiffy, so you'll be done before you know it!*

# Cozy Cover-ups

Spread a little warmth this season with these three cozy cover-ups. The adorable designs turn plain winter warmers into wonderful wardrobe classics for the holidays and all season long.

**Note:** For all projects, see Working on Waste Canvas, page 142.

**Ho Ho Ho** was stitched over a 7" x 17" piece of 8.5 mesh waste canvas on a purchased cardigan sweater. Six strands of floss were used for Cross Stitch and 2 for all other stitches. Refer to photo for placement.

**Let It Snow** was stitched over a 12" x 15" piece of 8.5 mesh waste canvas on a purchased sweater with top of design 2¼" from bottom of neckband. **Checkerboard Border only** was stitched over 11" x 4" pieces of 8.5 mesh waste canvas on sleeves 1" from beginning of cuff. Six strands of floss were used for Cross Stitch and 2 for all other stitches. **Also stitched** omitting Checkerboard Borders over a 9" x 10" piece of 10 mesh waste canvas on a purchased girl's dress. Five strands of floss were used for Cross Stitch and 2 strands for all other stitches.

**Noel** was stitched over a 12" x 8" piece of 8.5 mesh waste canvas on a purchased sweater with top of design 1½" from bottom of neckband. **Holly Border** was stitched over 11" x 4" pieces of 8.5 mesh waste canvas on sleeves 1" from beginning of cuff. Six strands of floss were used for Cross Stitch and 2 for all other stitches.

*Designed by Vicky Howard.*
*Needlework adaptation by Kathy Elrod.*

| X | DMC | ¼X | B'ST | JPC | COLOR |
|---|---|---|---|---|---|
| | blanc | | | 1001 | white |
| ■ | 310 | | ╱ | 8403 | black |
| ✕ | 321 | | ╱ | 3500 | dk red |
| C | 666 | | | 3046 | red |
| | 699 | | ╱ | 6228 | dk green |
| ★ | 700 | | | 6227 | green |
| | 701 | | | 6226 | lt green |
| ☆ | 721 | ◰ | ╱ | 2324 | orange |
| + | 794 | | | | blue |
| − | 911 | | | 6205 | dk yellow green |
| ◉ | 912 | | | 6205 | yellow green |
| ◯ | 928 | | | 7225 | grey |
| △ | 3733 | | | | pink |
| ● | 310 | | | black French Knot | |
| ◌ | Mill Hill Glass Pebble Bead #05025 Ruby Red | | | | |
| ◌ | Mill Hill Glass Pebble Bead #05081 Black Frost | | | | |
| ◉ | Mill Hill Glass Seed Bead #02013 Red Red | | | | |
| ◌ | Mill Hill Glass Seed Bead #00146 Light Blue | | | | |

LET IT SNOW (44w x 71h)

HO HO HO (20w x 110h)

NOEL (62w x 32h)  HOLLY BORDER (64w x 5h)

# Candy Cane Mice

*These cute little mice know that sharing the spirit of Christmas helps make the season bright. As you celebrate the holidays, why not wear this fun sweatshirt and spread some Yuletide cheer of your own!*

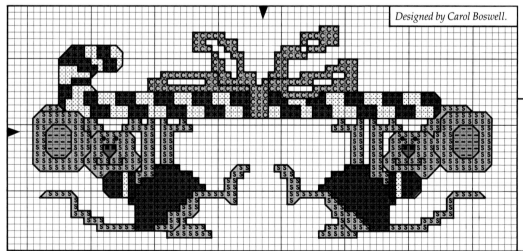

*Designed by Carol Boswell.*

**Christmas is Sharing was** stitched over a 13" x 8" piece of 8.5 mesh waste canvas on a purchased sweatshirt. Six strands of floss were used for Cross Stitch and 2 for Backstitch and French Knots. See Working on Waste Canvas, page 142.

### CHRISTMAS IS SHARING (72w x 32h)

| X | DMC | ¼X | B'ST | JPC | COLOR |
|---|-----|-----|------|------|-------|
| (blanc) | blanc | | | 1001 | white |
| ■ | 310 | | / | 8403 | black |
| S | 318 | | | 8511 | grey |
| ✳ | 321 | | | 3500 | red |
| C | 699 | | | 6228 | green |
| - | 776 | | | 3281 | pink |
| ● | 310 | | black French Knot | | |

# Santa Button Blouse

*Button covers featuring jolly old St. Nick and plaid ribbon accents make this holiday blouse extra-festive. Worn at work or play, this easy fashion will help you show your Christmas spirit!*

1. Wash, dry, and press a $^7/_8$"w plaid ribbon and a white cotton blouse with collar and cuffed sleeves.
2. (**Note:** Use fabric glue for all gluing unless otherwise indicated. Refer to photo for Steps 2 - 5.) For ribbon trim on front of blouse, measure 1 side of front opening; add $^1/_2$". Cut a length of ribbon the determined measurement. For ribbon trim on cuffs, measure around top of 1 cuff; add 1". Cut 2 lengths of ribbon the determined measurement. Apply fray preventative to ribbon ends; allow to dry.
3. For front of blouse, place ribbon length along front opening over buttonholes with one end of ribbon length even with collar; use fabric glue to glue in place. Fold ribbon end at bottom of blouse to wrong side; glue in place. Stitching along long edges of ribbon, sew ribbon to blouse.
4. For each cuff, center one ribbon length on cuff; glue in place. Fold ends of ribbon to inside of cuff; glue in place. Stitching along long edges of ribbon, sew ribbon to cuff.
5. Use fabric marking pen to mark original placement of buttonholes on ribbon. Stitching through ribbon, work a buttonhole at each mark. Cut buttonholes open.

6. Trace circle pattern onto tracing paper; cut out.
7. (**Note:** Follow Steps 7 - 9 for each button cover.) Stitch design on a 4" x 4" piece of White Aida (11 ct) using 2 strands of floss for Cross Stitch and 1 for Backstitch and French Knots.
8. Trim stitched piece to $^1/_2$" from design on all sides. Cut white cotton fabric for backing same size as stitched piece. Using foam brush, apply fabric stiffener to back of stitched piece; place stitched piece on backing fabric, smoothing stitched piece while pressing fabrics together. Allow to dry. Apply stiffener

to backing fabric; allow to dry. Apply stiffener to front of stitched piece; allow to dry.
9. With design centered, use circle pattern to cut out stitched piece. Use pattern to cut one circle from poster board. Glue stitched piece to poster board circle. Hot glue button cover hardware to center of poster board circle.
10. Attach button covers to buttons. Tie a length of ribbon into a bow around neck of blouse.

*Designed by Ann Townsend.*

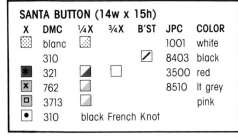

**SANTA BUTTON (14w x 15h)**

| X | DMC | ¼X | ¾X | B'ST | JPC | COLOR |
|---|-----|-----|-----|------|-----|-------|
| ▨ | blanc | ▨ | | | 1001 | white |
| | 310 | | | ◪ | 8403 | black |
| ✳ | 321 | ◪ | ☐ | | 3500 | red |
| ✕ | 762 | ◪ | | | 8510 | lt grey |
| ▢ | 3713 | ◪ | | | | pink |
| ● | 310 | | black French Knot | | | |

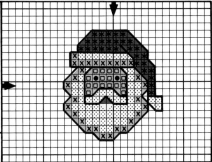

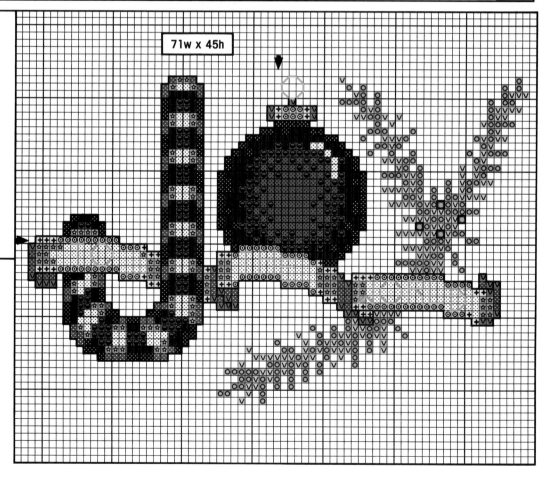

# Joyful Sweatshirt

*Our joyous sweatshirt will become a favorite for holiday get-togethers, Christmas caroling, or other Yuletide fun. Decked with a merry message, it's sure to spread seasonal cheer.*

| X | DMC | B'ST | ANC. | COLOR |
|---|---|---|---|---|
| ░ | blanc | | 2 | white |
| | 310 | ✔ | 403 | black |
| ◨ | 321 | | 9046 | red |
| ▨ | 415 | | 398 | dk grey |
| ■ | 498 | | 1005 | dk red |
| ▨ | 666 | | 46 | lt red |
| ◉ | 700 | ✔ * | 228 | dk green |
| ⊙ | 725 | | 305 | yellow |
| ★ | 762 | | 234 | grey |
| V | 782 | | 308 | dk gold |
| + | 783 | ✔ * | 307 | gold |
| ▨ | 815 | | 43 | vy dk red |
| V | 906 | | 256 | green |
| ● | Mill Hill Seed Bead - #02013 | | | |

\* Use 4 strands for Backstitch.

**Joy:** Stitched over a 14" x 11" piece of 8.5 mesh waste canvas on a purchased sweatshirt. Six strands of floss used for Cross Stitch and 2 for Backstitch, unless otherwise indicated in color key. See Working on Waste Canvas, page 142.

To attach beads, refer to chart for bead placement and sew bead in place using 1 strand of DMC 321 floss and a fine needle that will pass through bead.

*Design by Vicky Howard.*
*Needlework adaptation by Jane Chandler.*

71w x 45h

# Herald Angel

*With trumpet sound, this angel joyfully heralds the Christmas season. What a glorious design for a holiday sweater!*

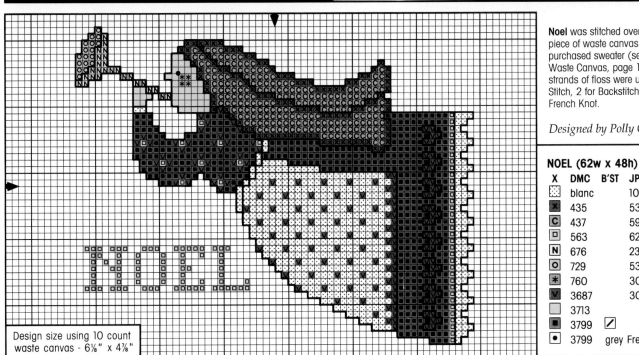

**Noel** was stitched over a 10" x 9" piece of waste canvas (10 ct) on a purchased sweater (see Working on Waste Canvas, page 142). Six strands of floss were used for Cross Stitch, 2 for Backstitch, and 2 for French Knot.

*Designed by Polly Carbonari.*

Design size using 10 count waste canvas - 6⅛" x 4⅞"

**NOEL (62w x 48h)**

| X | DMC | B'ST | JPC | COLOR |
|---|-----|------|-----|-------|
| ▨ | blanc | | 1001 | white |
| ✖ | 435 | | 5371 | tan |
| C | 437 | | 5942 | lt tan |
| ▢ | 563 | | 6210 | green |
| N | 676 | | 2305 | lt gold |
| O | 729 | | 5363 | gold |
| ✳ | 760 | | 3069 | pink |
| V | 3687 | | 3088 | rose |
| ▨ | 3713 | | | flesh |
| ▪ | 3799 | ∕ | | grey |
| • | 3799 | | | grey French Knot |

# Christmas Socks

*Quick and easy to stitch, these Christmas socks make great stocking stuffers! There's a snowman, a pair of Santas, an angel, a reindeer, and lots more.*

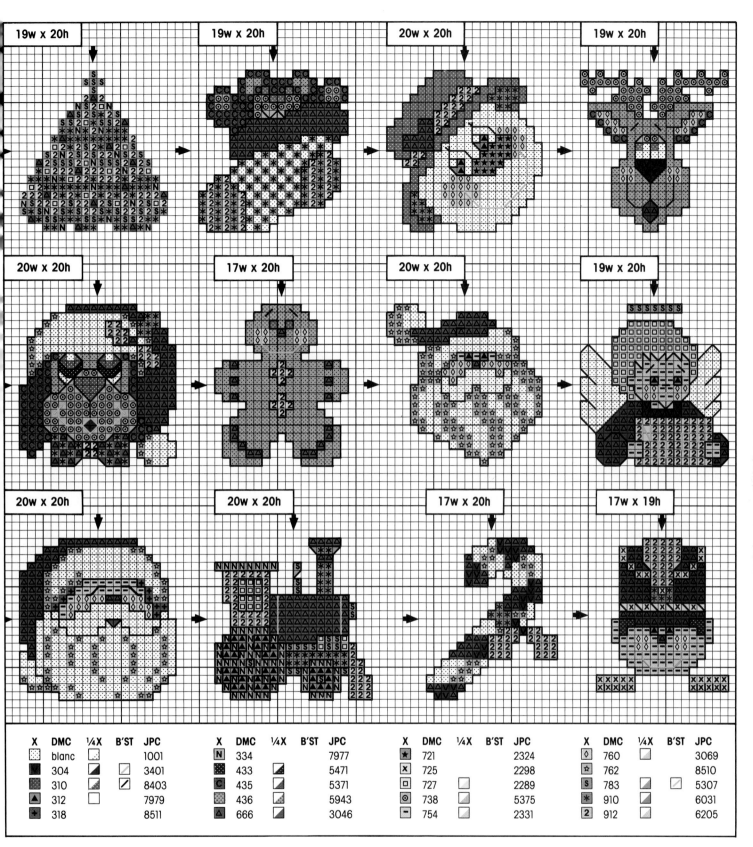

| X | DMC | ¼X | B'ST | JPC | | X | DMC | ¼X | B'ST | JPC | | X | DMC | ¼X | B'ST | JPC | | X | DMC | ¼X | B'ST | JPC |
|---|-----|-----|------|-----|---|---|-----|-----|------|-----|---|---|-----|-----|------|-----|---|---|-----|-----|------|-----|
| | blanc | | | 1001 | | N | 334 | | | 7977 | | ★ | 721 | | | 2324 | | ◊ | 760 | | | 3069 |
| | 304 | | | 3401 | | | 433 | | | 5471 | | X | 725 | | | 2298 | | ☆ | 762 | | | 8510 |
| | 310 | | | 8403 | | C | 435 | | | 5371 | | □ | 727 | | | 2289 | | S | 783 | | | 5307 |
| ▲ | 312 | | | 7979 | | | 436 | | | 5943 | | ☉ | 738 | | | 5375 | | ✳ | 910 | | | 6031 |
| ✦ | 318 | | | 8511 | | △ | 666 | | | 3046 | | — | 754 | | | 2331 | | 2 | 912 | | | 6205 |

Each design was stitched over a 3" square of 14 mesh waste canvas on the cuff of a sock (see Working on Waste Canvas, page 142). Three strands of floss were used for Cross Stitch, 2 for 304 and 783 Backstitch, and 1 for 310 Backstitch.

*Designed by Terrie Lee Steinmeyer ©1992.*

49

# Reindeer Noel

*This tiny quartet offers a simple, but heartfelt, Christmas greeting. We stitched the design on a child's sweatshirt so that your little "dear" can spread holiday cheer.*

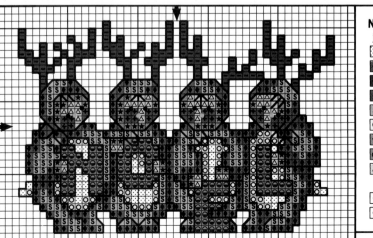

**NOEL (45w x 29h)**

| X | DMC | ¼X | B'ST | JPC | COLOR |
|---|-----|-----|------|-----|-------|
| ▨ | blanc | | | 1001 | white |
| ✳ | 353 | ◩ | | 3006 | dk flesh |
| ■ | 433 | ◩ | | 5471 | dk brown |
| ◆ | 435 | ◩ | | 5371 | brown |
| S | 437 | ◩ | | 5942 | lt brown |
| ○ | 712 | | | 5387 | cream |
| ★ | 754 | ◩ | | 2331 | flesh |
| ◉ | 911 | | | 6205 | green |
| △ | 948 | ◩ | | 2331 | lt flesh |
| | 3371 | | ◪ | 5478 | brown black |
| ● | 321 | | | red French Knot | |
| ⊙ | 3371 | | | brown black French Knot | |

**Noel:** Stitched over a 10" x 8" piece of 8.5 mesh waste canvas on a purchased sweatshirt (see Working on Waste Canvas, page 142). Six strands of floss used for Cross Stitch and 2 strands for all other stitches.

*Designed by Lorraine Birmingham.*

50

# Merry Mouse

*Our merry mouse turns a plain adult-size tee into a cute and comfy nightshirt for boys or girls. The fun sleepwear is just right for nestling snug in their beds on Christmas Eve.*

| CHRISTMAS MOUSE (45w x 53h) | | | | |
|---|---|---|---|---|
| X | DMC | ¼X | B'ST | ANC. | COLOR |
| | blanc | | | 2 | white |
| | 310 | | ✔ | 403 | black |
| O | 318 | | | 399 | grey |
| | 666 | | | 46 | red |
| + | 910 | | | 229 | green |
| – | 3716 | | | 25 | pink |

**Christmas Mouse** was stitched over a 9" x 10" piece of 10 mesh waste canvas on a purchased blue T-Shirt. Five strands of floss were used for Cross Stitch and 2 for Backstitch. The design was centered horizontally with the top edge of the design 1" from the bottom of the neckband. See Working on Waste Canvas, page 142.

*Design by Carol Boswell.*

| CHRISTMAS MOUSE (45w x 53h) | | | |
|---|---|---|---|
| 14 count | 3¼" | x | 3⅞" |
| 16 count | 2⅞" | x | 3⅜" |
| 18 count | 2½" | x | 3" |
| 22 count | 2⅛" | x | 2½" |

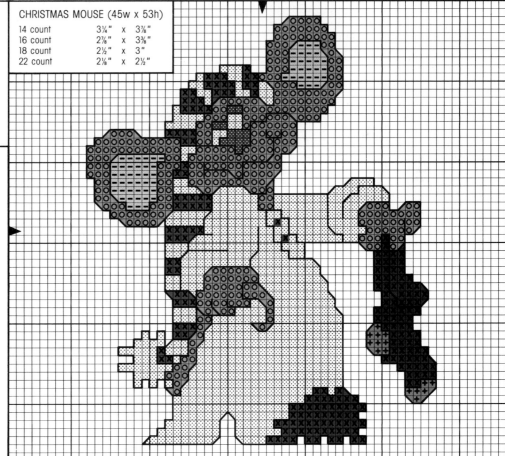

# "Seasoned" Greetings

*The aromas of Christmas add to the warmth of the celebration. When you wear this whimsical apron, you'll be ready to serve up "seasoned" greetings to all who share your holidays.*

**Seasoned Greetings** was stitched over an 11" x 15" piece of 10 mesh waste canvas on a purchased apron. Five strands of floss were used for Cross Stitch and 2 for Backstitch.

*Original artwork by Vicky Howard. Needlework adaptation by Mike Vickery.*

**Working on Waste Canvas:** Waste canvas is a special canvas that provides an evenweave grid for placing stitches on fabric. After the design is worked over the canvas, the canvas threads are removed, leaving the design on the fabric. The canvas is available in several mesh sizes.
1. Cover edges of canvas with masking tape.
2. Find desired stitching area on apron and mark center of area with a pin.
3. Match center of canvas to pin. Use the blue threads in canvas to place canvas straight on apron; pin canvas to apron. Baste all thicknesses together.
4. Place apron in a screw-type hoop. We recommend a hoop that is large enough to encircle entire design.
5. Using a sharp needle, work design, stitching from large holes to large holes.
6. Trim canvas to within ¾" of design. Dampen canvas until it becomes limp. Pull out canvas threads one at a time using tweezers.

**SEASONED GREETINGS**

| | | |
|---|---|---|
| 14 count | 4¾" | x 7⅞" |
| 16 count | 4⅛" | x 6⅞" |
| 18 count | 3¾" | x 6⅛" |
| 22 count | 3" | x 5" |

**SEASONED GREETINGS (66w x 109h)**

| X | DMC | ¼X | ¾X | B'ST | ANC. | COLOR |
|---|---|---|---|---|---|---|
| ▨ | blanc | ▨ | | | 2 | white |
| ▨ | 310 | | ◣ | ╱ | 403 | black |
| ◉ | 304 | | ◤ | | 1006 | dk red |
| ▨ | 321 | ◢ | | | 9046 | red |
| V | 434 | ◢ | | | 310 | brown |
| ◉ | 436 | ◢ | | | 1045 | lt brown |
| ■ | 498 | ◢ | | | 1005 | vy dk red |
| − | 666 | ◢ | | | 46 | lt red |
| ☆ | 762 | ◢ | | | 234 | grey |
| ■ | 801 | ◤ | | | 359 | dk brown |
| ◆ | 909 | ◢ | | | 923 | dk green |
| X | 911 | ◢ | | | 205 | green |

53

# Reindeer Sweatshirt

*This playful reindeer will capture your heart as he bounds through an evergreen forest. Designed by Polly Carbonari, the traditional motif turns everyday sportswear into a fun Christmas top. You'll enjoy this colorful sweatshirt long after the holidays!*

**Reindeer** was stitched over a 14" x 9" piece of waste canvas (8.5 ct) on a purchased sweatshirt (see Working on Waste Canvas, page 142). Six strands of floss were used for Cross Stitch.

*Designed by Polly Carbonari.*

Design size using 8.5 count waste canvas — 9½ x 4⅝.

**REINDEER (80w x 39h)**

| X | DMC | ANC. | COLOR |
|---|-----|------|-------|
| ○ | ecru | 0926 | ecru |
| ■ | 310 | 0403 | black |
| ✳ | 321 | 047 | red |
| □ | 433 | 0371 | brown |
| ✕ | 436 | 0363 | tan |
| – | 562 | 0205 | green |
| △ | 648 | 0398 | grey |

# Under the Mistletoe

*Standing under the mistletoe, our cute teddy bear sneaks a kiss from a dainty dolly. This sweatshirt is sure to bring fun to the holidays!*

## CHRISTMAS KISS (40w x 68h)

| X | DMC | B'ST | ¼X | JPC | COLOR |
|---|------|------|-----|------|--------|
|   | blanc |   |   | 1001 | white |
|   | 312 |   |   | 7979 | blue |
|   | 321 |   |   | 3500 | red |
|   | 322 |   |   | 7978 | lt blue |
|   | 436 |   |   | 5943 | brown |
|   | 437 |   |   | 5942 | lt brown |
|   | 666 |   |   | 3046 | lt red |
|   | 738 |   |   | 5375 | dk tan |
|   | 739 |   |   | 5369 | tan |
|   | 744 |   |   | 2293 | yellow |
|   | 745 |   |   | 2296 | lt yellow |
|   | 754 |   |   | 2331 | peach |
|   | 760 |   |   | 3069 | pink |
|   | 910 |   |   | 6031 | green |
|   | 3072 |   |   | 6005 | grey |
|   | 3371 |   |   | 5478 | dk brown |
|   | 321 |   |   |   | red French Knot |
|   | 910 |   |   |   | green Lazy Daisy Stitch |

**Christmas Kiss** was stitched over a 9" x 12" piece of waste canvas (8.5 ct) on a purchased sweatshirt (see Working on Waste Canvas, page 142). Six strands of floss were used for Cross Stitch, 2 for Backstitch, 2 for French Knots, and 2 for Lazy Daisy Stitches. A ribbon bow was tacked to sweatshirt (see photo).

*Design adapted from a Family Line, Inc. greeting card. ©1983*
*Anna Grossnickle Hines, Artist.*

Design size using 8.5 count waste canvas — 4¾" x 8"

# Merry Nightwear

*Perfect for Christmas Eve, these festive nightclothes are a breeze to create using purchased gowns, nightshirts, and pajamas. The whole family can wait for Santa Claus in style with this merry sleepwear.*

'Twas the night...

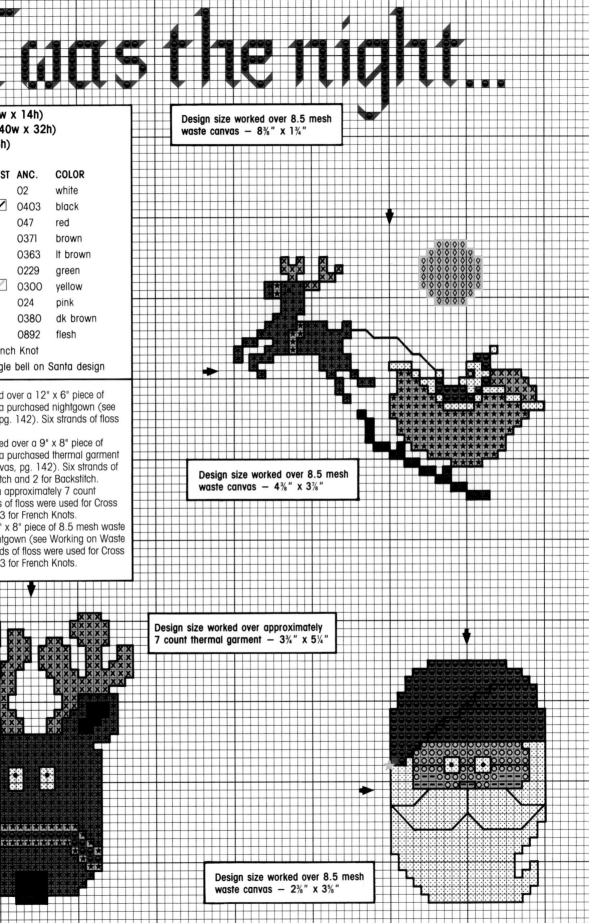

**TWAS THE NIGHT** (71w x 14h)
**SANTA AND SLEIGH** (40w x 32h)
**REINDEER** (26w x 36h)
**SANTA** (20w x 30h)

| X | DMC | ¾X | B'ST | ANC. | COLOR |
|---|-----|-----|------|------|-------|
| ░ | blanc | | | 02 | white |
| | 310 | | ◩ | 0403 | black |
| ◉ | 321 | ◨ | | 047 | red |
| ✳ | 433 | | | 0371 | brown |
| ✕ | 436 | | | 0363 | lt brown |
| ★ | 700 | | | 0229 | green |
| ◇ | 745 | | ◩ | 0300 | yellow |
| — | 776 | | | 024 | pink |
| ■ | 838 | | | 0380 | dk brown |
| ◎ | 948 | | | 0892 | flesh |
| ● | 310 | | black French Knot | | |
| ✦ | placement of jingle bell on Santa design | | | | |

**'Twas The Night** was stitched over a 12" x 6" piece of 8.5 mesh waste canvas on a purchased nightgown (see Working on Waste Canvas, pg. 142). Six strands of floss were used for Cross Stitch.
**Santa And Sleigh** was stitched over a 9" x 8" piece of 8.5 mesh waste canvas on a purchased thermal garment (see Working on Waste Canvas, pg. 142). Six strands of floss were used for Cross Stitch and 2 for Backstitch.
**Reindeer** was stitched on an approximately 7 count thermal garment. Six strands of floss were used for Cross Stitch, 2 for Backstitch, and 3 for French Knots.
**Santa** was stitched over a 6" x 8" piece of 8.5 mesh waste canvas on a purchased nightgown (see Working on Waste Canvas, pg. 142). Six strands of floss were used for Cross Stitch, 2 for Backstitch, and 3 for French Knots.

Design size worked over 8.5 mesh waste canvas — 8⅜" x 1¾"

Design size worked over 8.5 mesh waste canvas — 4⅜" x 3⅞"

Design size worked over approximately 7 count thermal garment — 3¾" x 5¼"

Design size worked over 8.5 mesh waste canvas — 2⅜" x 3⅝"

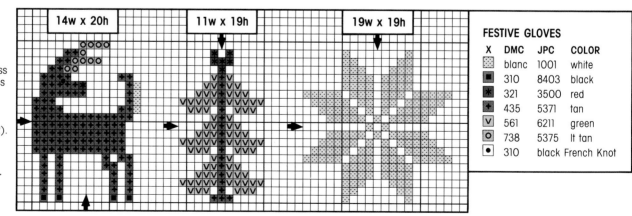

# Festive Gloves

*With these cute designs and purchased gloves, you can create something special for everyone on your gift list. The gloves will make family and friends feel warm and appreciated all winter long!*

Each design was stitched over a 2" square of waste canvas (10 ct) on purchased gloves. Four strands of floss were used for Cross Stitch and 3 for French Knot (See Working on Waste Canvas, page 142).

*Designed by Polly Carbonari.*

14w x 20h    11w x 19h    19w x 19h

**FESTIVE GLOVES**

| X | DMC | JPC | COLOR |
|---|-----|-----|-------|
| ▧ | blanc | 1001 | white |
| ■ | 310 | 8403 | black |
| ✶ | 321 | 3500 | red |
| ✚ | 435 | 5371 | tan |
| V | 561 | 6211 | green |
| O | 738 | 5375 | lt tan |
| ● | 310 | | black French Knot |

# Snowman Tunic

*A plain white tunic becomes a winter favorite when you stitch our friendly snowmen along the bottom edge. The shirt will keep you from feeling the chill in the air — and the frosty fellows will keep you smiling, too!*

**Snowman Border** (for front of tunic only) was stitched over a 27" x 6" piece of 10 mesh waste canvas on a purchased white knit tunic (see Working on Waste Canvas, page 142). Four strands of floss were used for Cross Stitch and 2 for Backstitch. Repeat design as desired.

*Designed by Ann Townsend.*

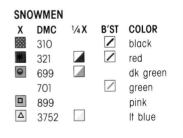

**SNOWMEN**

| X | DMC | 1/4 X | B'ST | COLOR |
|---|-----|-------|------|-------|
| ▓ | 310 | | ✓ | black |
| ✳ | 321 | ◪ | ✓ | red |
| ◉ | 699 | ◪ | | dk green |
| | 701 | ◪ | ✓ | green |
| ▣ | 899 | | | pink |
| △ | 3752 | ▢ | | lt blue |

# Holiday Pals

*During the hustle and bustle of the Yuletide season, our chubby Santa and his gentle reindeer pause to share a simple Yuletide message. Stitched over waste canvas, the design is easy to add to a sweatshirt.*

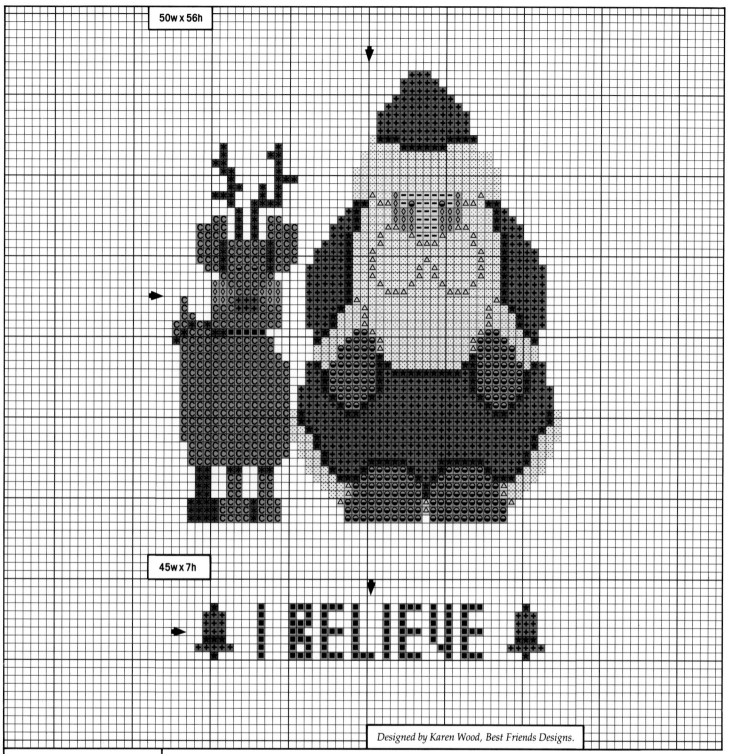

**50w x 56h**

**45w x 7h**

I BELIEVE

*Designed by Karen Wood, Best Friends Designs.*

| X | DMC | JPC | COLOR |
|---|---|---|---|
| ⠿ | blanc | 1001 | white |
| ◉ | 310 | 8403 | black |
| ✚ | 321 | 3500 | red |
| ◇ | 353 | 3006 | rose |
| ◼ | 498 | 3410 | dk red |
| ◼ | 561 | 6211 | green |
| — | 754 | 2331 | peach |
| ✳ | 839 | 5360 | dk brown |
| C | 841 | 5376 | lt brown |
| △ | 842 | 5933 | tan |

**Santa and Reindeer** was stitched over an 11" x 14½" piece of 8.5 mesh waste canvas on a purchased ivory sweatshirt (see Working on Waste Canvas, page 142). Referring to photo for placement, stitch design repeating "I Believe" twice below Santa and Reindeer. Six strands of floss were used for Cross Stitch.

Refer to photo for placement and tack a 3" length of 003HL Kreinik Balger® #32 Braid to reindeer's collar and Santa's mitten. Insert a 1" length of braid through an 8mm jingle bell; tack braid to reindeer's collar.

# Ho-Ho-Ho Sweatshirt

*Children will love this sweatshirt featuring a playful Santa juggling pom-pom snowballs. The words "Ho-Ho-Ho" spread the whimsical holiday spirit.*

**"HO-HO-HO"** was stitched over an 11" x 8" piece of 10 mesh waste canvas on a purchased sweatshirt (see Working on Waste Canvas, pg. 142). Five strands of floss were used for Cross Stitch and 2 for Backstitch. For snowballs, refer to photo to glue pom-poms to shirt.

*Designed by Ann Townsend.*

Design size worked over 10 mesh waste canvas — 7" x 4".

### "HO-HO-HO" (69w x 40h)

| X | DMC | ¼X | ¾X | B'ST | JPC | COLOR |
|---|-----|-----|-----|------|-----|-------|
| | blanc | | | | 1001 | white |
| | 310 | | | | 8403 | black |
| | 321 | | | | 3500 | red |
| | 699 | | | | 6228 | dk green |
| | 701 | | | | 6226 | green |
| | 762 | | | | 8510 | lt grey |
| | 899 | | | | 3282 | pink |
| | 3713 | | | | | lt pink |

# Country Santas

*These tiny country Santas send "Merry Christmas" greetings. The cute design works up in no time, but your enjoyment will last throughout the holiday season.*

**Country Santas** was stitched over a 14" x 9" piece of waste canvas (8.5 ct) on a purchased sweatshirt (see Working on Waste Canvas, page 142). Six strands of floss were used for Cross Stitch and 2 for Backstitch and French Knots.

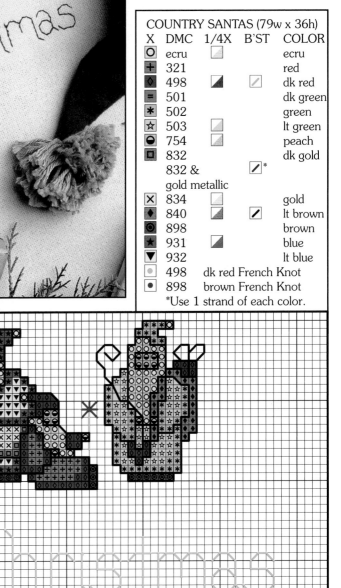

| X | DMC | 1/4X | B'ST | COLOR |
|---|---|---|---|---|
| O | ecru | | | ecru |
| + | 321 | | | red |
| ◈ | 498 | ◪ | ◿ | dk red |
| = | 501 | | | dk green |
| * | 502 | | | green |
| ☆ | 503 | ◪ | | lt green |
| ◒ | 754 | ◪ | | peach |
| ▣ | 832 | | | dk gold |
| | 832 & | | ◿* | |
| | gold metallic | | | |
| ⊠ | 834 | ◪ | | gold |
| ◆ | 840 | ◪ | ◿ | lt brown |
| ◎ | 898 | | | brown |
| ★ | 931 | ◪ | | blue |
| ▼ | 932 | | | lt blue |
| ○ | 498 | | | dk red French Knot |
| ● | 898 | | | brown French Knot |

*Use 1 strand of each color.

*Designed by Julia Bailey.*

**COUNTRY SANTAS (79w x 36h)**

# Buttoned-Up Tree

Adorned with buttons in a variety of colors and sizes, a simple feather tree lends an old-fashioned air to a plain sweatshirt.

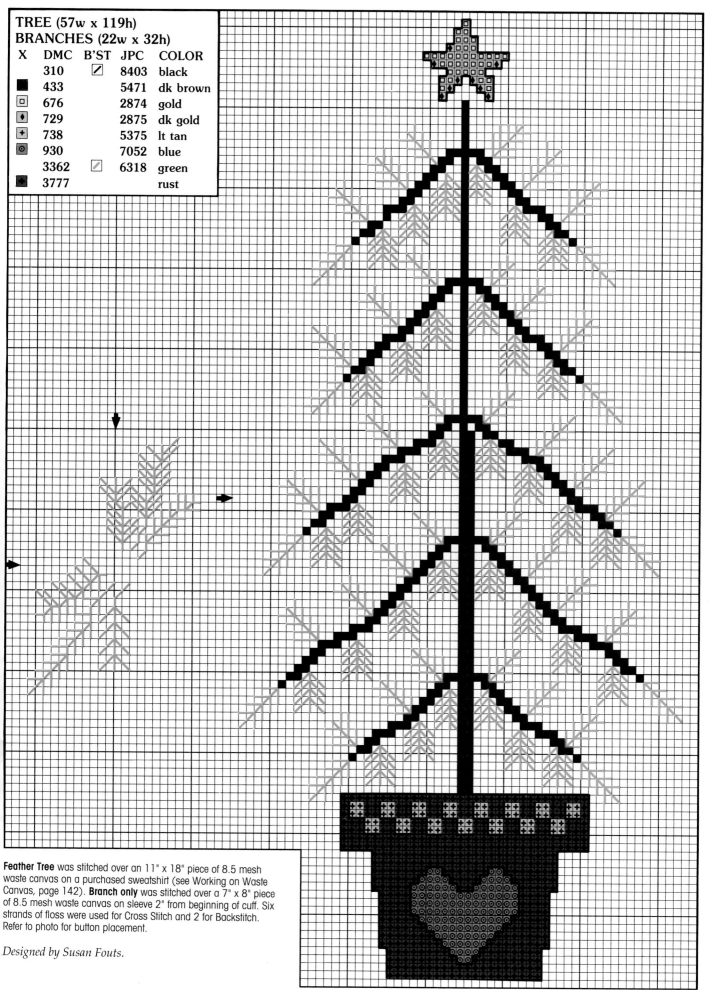

**TREE (57w x 119h)**
**BRANCHES (22w x 32h)**

| X | DMC | B'ST | JPC | COLOR |
|---|-----|------|-----|-------|
| | 310 | ∕ | 8403 | black |
| ■ | 433 | | 5471 | dk brown |
| ▣ | 676 | | 2874 | gold |
| ◆ | 729 | | 2875 | dk gold |
| ✚ | 738 | | 5375 | lt tan |
| ◉ | 930 | | 7052 | blue |
| | 3362 | ∕ | 6318 | green |
| ◈ | 3777 | | | rust |

**Feather Tree** was stitched over an 11" x 18" piece of 8.5 mesh waste canvas on a purchased sweatshirt (see Working on Waste Canvas, page 142). **Branch only** was stitched over a 7" x 8" piece of 8.5 mesh waste canvas on sleeve 2" from beginning of cuff. Six strands of floss were used for Cross Stitch and 2 for Backstitch. Refer to photo for button placement.

*Designed by Susan Fouts.*

# Teddy Bear Pinafore

*Your favorite little girl will look precious in this pretty pinafore. We made ours, but you can easily attach a cross-stitched panel to a purchased one in no time. The adorable teddy bears and heart borders give the outfit a touch of Yuletide cheer.*

**Hearts and Bears** was stitched on a 10" x 9" piece of White Aida (14 ct). Three strands of floss were used for Cross Stitch, 1 for Backstitch, and 3 for French Knots. Use a pinafore pattern of your choice, or attach stitched piece over the insert of a purchased pinafore.

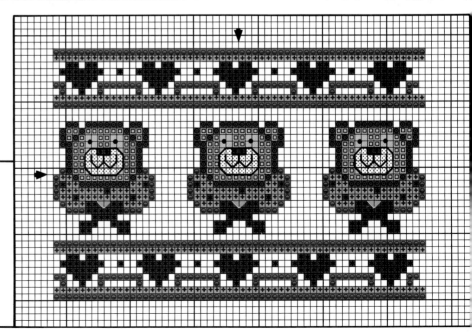

### HEARTS AND BEARS (58w x 38h)

| X | DMC | ¼ X | B'ST | JPC | COLOR |
|---|---|---|---|---|---|
| | blanc | | | 1001 | white |
| | 321 | | | 3500 | red |
| | 433 | | | 5471 | dk tan |
| | 436 | | | 5943 | tan |
| | 699 | | | 6228 | dk green |
| | 702 | | | 6239 | lt green |
| | 3371 | | | 5478 | dk brown |
| | 3371 | dk brown French Knot | | | |

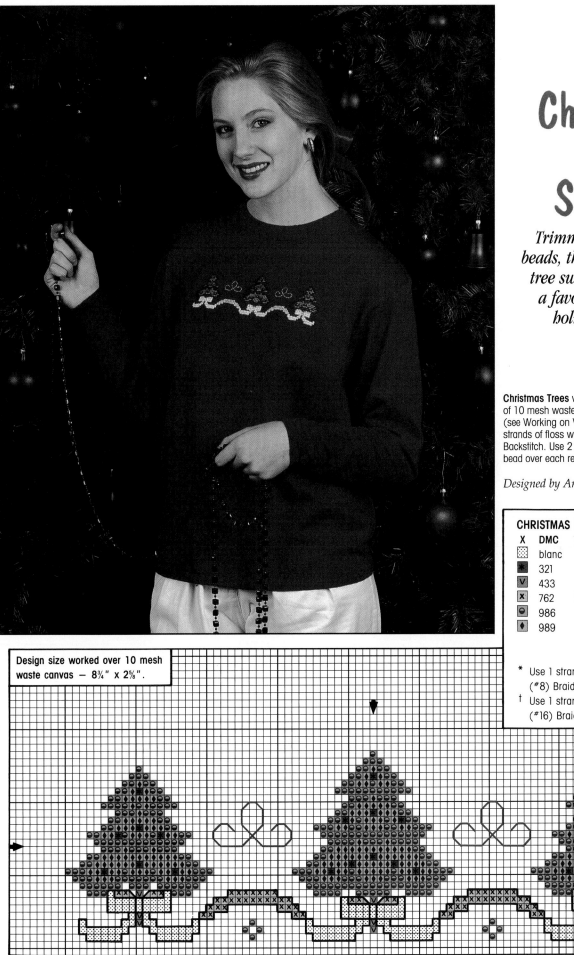

# Christmas Tree Sweater

*Trimmed with red glass beads, this pretty Christmas tree sweater is sure to be a favorite part of your holiday wardrobe.*

**Christmas Trees** was stitched over a 13" x 7" piece of 10 mesh waste canvas on a purchased sweater (see Working on Waste Canvas, page 142). Four strands of floss were used for Cross Stitch and 2 for Backstitch. Use 2 strands of red floss to sew 1 red bead over each red stitch in trees.

*Designed by Ann Townsend.*

**CHRISTMAS TREES (87w x 26h)**

| X | DMC | ¼X | B'ST | JPC | COLOR |
|---|-----|-----|------|-----|-------|
| ▨ | blanc | | | 1001 | white |
| ✹ | 321 | | | 3500 | red |
| V | 433 | | | 5471 | lt brown |
| x | 762 | ▨ | | 8510 | lt grey |
| ◉ | 986 | | | 6021 | dk green |
| ◆ | 989 | | | 6266 | lt green |
| | | | ╱* | | gold |
| | | | ╱† | | gold |

\* Use 1 strand of Kreinik Balger Fine (#8) Braid #002 gold.

† Use 1 strand of Kreinik Balger Medium (#16) Braid #002 gold.

**Design size worked over 10 mesh waste canvas — 8¾" x 2⅝".**

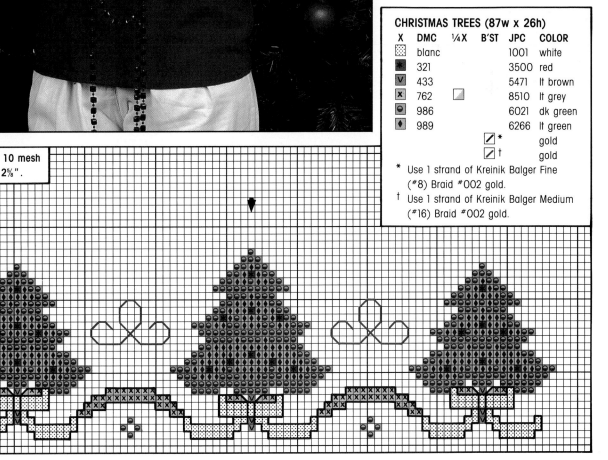

# Snow Pal

*Amid a flurry of snowflakes and pearls, this frosty fellow makes a jolly addition to a sweatshirt. This cheery top can be worn at Christmas and all winter long, too!*

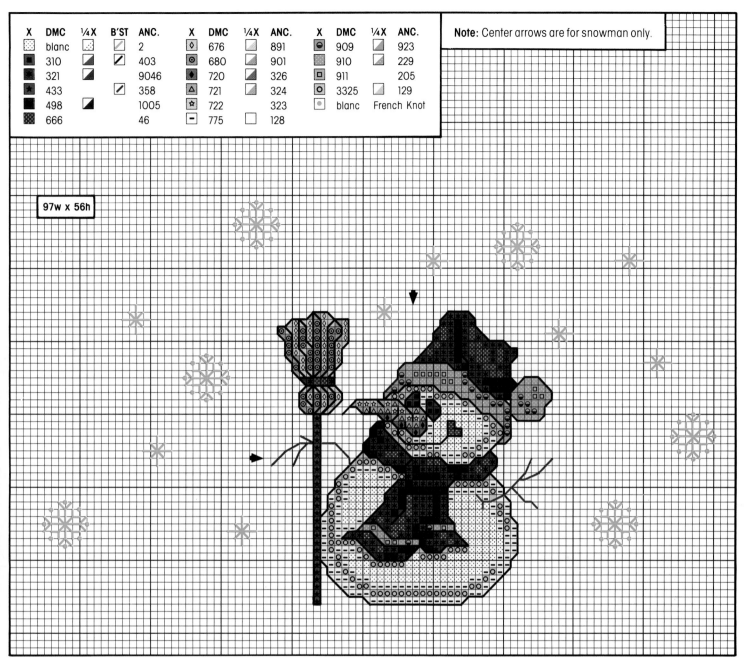

| X | DMC | ¼X | B'ST | ANC. | | X | DMC | ¼X | ANC. | | X | DMC | ¼X | ANC. |
|---|---|---|---|---|---|---|---|---|---|---|---|---|---|---|
| ▫ | blanc | ▫ | ◪ | 2 | | ◇ | 676 | ◪ | 891 | | ◉ | 909 | ◪ | 923 |
| ■ | 310 | ◪ | ◪ | 403 | | ⊙ | 680 | ◪ | 901 | | ◉ | 910 | ◪ | 229 |
| ■ | 321 | ◪ | | 9046 | | ◆ | 720 | ◪ | 326 | | ▣ | 911 | | 205 |
| ★ | 433 | | ◪ | 358 | | △ | 721 | ◪ | 324 | | ◎ | 3325 | ◪ | 129 |
| ■ | 498 | ◪ | | 1005 | | ☆ | 722 | | 323 | | • | blanc | French Knot | |
| ▦ | 666 | | | 46 | | ⊟ | 775 | | 128 | | | | | |

**Note:** Center arrows are for snowman only.

**97w x 56h**

Design was stitched over a 15" x 12" piece of 8.5 mesh waste canvas on a purchased sweatshirt. Six strands of floss were used for Cross Stitch, 4 for blanc Backstitch and French Knots, and 2 for all other Backstitch. Refer to photo to sew pearls to shirt.

**Working on Waste Canvas:** Waste canvas is a special canvas that provides an evenweave grid for placing stitches on fabric. After the design is worked over the canvas, the canvas threads are removed, leaving the design on the fabric. The canvas is available in several mesh sizes.
1. Cover edges of canvas with masking tape. When working on lightweight fabric, cut a piece of lightweight, non-fusible interfacing the same size as canvas to provide a firm stitching base.
2. Find desired stitching area on garment and mark center of area with a pin. Match center of canvas to pin on garment. With canvas threads straight, pin canvas to garment; pin interfacing to wrong side. Baste all three thicknesses together as shown in **Fig. 1**.

3. Using a sharp needle, work design, stitching from large holes to large holes.
4. Trim canvas to within ¾" of design. Dampen canvas until it becomes limp. Using tweezers, pull out canvas threads one at a time (**Fig. 2**).
5. Trim interfacing close to design.

**Fig. 1**

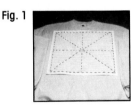

**Fig. 2**

*Designed by Marianne Wourms.*

# Jingle Bell Bear

*Ready for caroling, this bear rings in the season with holiday spirit, and his gleeful grin reminds us of the fun of Christmas. Stitched on a sweatshirt, the happy teddy will spread cheer wherever you go.*

*Designed by Carol Boswell.*

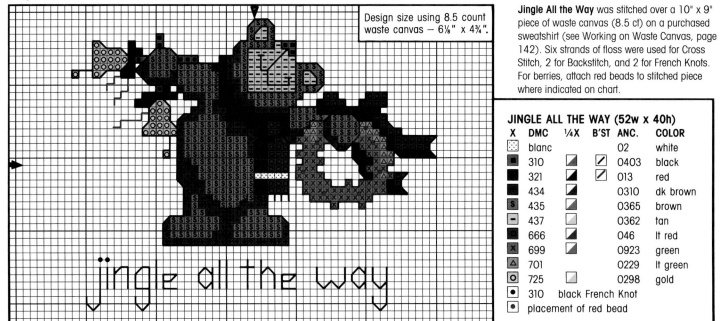

Design size using 8.5 count waste canvas — 6⅛" x 4¾".

**Jingle All the Way** was stitched over a 10" x 9" piece of waste canvas (8.5 ct) on a purchased sweatshirt (see Working on Waste Canvas, page 142). Six strands of floss were used for Cross Stitch, 2 for Backstitch, and 2 for French Knots. For berries, attach red beads to stitched piece where indicated on chart.

### JINGLE ALL THE WAY (52w x 40h)

| X | DMC | ¼X | B'ST | ANC. | COLOR |
|---|-----|-----|------|------|-------|
| ▦ | blanc | | | 02 | white |
| ■ | 310 | ◪ | ◹ | 0403 | black |
| ■ | 321 | ◪ | ◹ | 013 | red |
| ■ | 434 | ◪ | | 0310 | dk brown |
| S | 435 | ◪ | | 0365 | brown |
| - | 437 | ◩ | | 0362 | tan |
| ■ | 666 | ◪ | | 046 | lt red |
| X | 699 | ◪ | | 0923 | green |
| △ | 701 | ◪ | | 0229 | lt green |
| ⦿ | 725 | ◪ | | 0298 | gold |
| ⬤ | 310 | | | black French Knot | |
| ⦿ | placement of red bead | | | | |

# Santa's Helper Tote

*A must for every official "Santa's Helper," this cute tote bag will hold lots of surprises for special friends. The carryall lets you show off your stitching in a big way, and it will be handy during the holidays!*

**Santa's Helper** was stitched on a prefinished Herta (6 ct) Big Bag. Eight strands of floss were used for Cross Stitch, 2 for Backstitch, and 2 for French Knots.

*Design by Carol Emmer.*

### SANTA'S HELPER (72w x 36h)

| X | DMC | ¼X | B'ST | ANC. | COLOR |
|---|-----|-----|------|------|-------|
| ⊡ | blanc | ⊡ | | 02 | white |
| ■ | 304 | | | 047 | dk red |
| | 310 | | ╱ | 0403 | black |
| ◉ | 312 | | | 0979 | blue |
| ✕ | 321 | | ╱ | 013 | red |
| + | 334 | | | 0977 | lt blue |
| ▣ | 700 | | ╱ | 0228 | green |
| ○ | 725 | □ | | 0306 | yellow |
| – | 754 | ◪ | | 4146 | flesh |
| △ | 760 | | | 09 | pink |
| ✳ | 783 | ◩ | | 0307 | dk yellow |
| ● | 310 | | | black French Knot | |

### SANTA'S HELPER (72w x 36h)

| | | |
|---|---|---|
| Aida 11 | 6⅝" | x 3⅜" |
| Aida 14 | 5¼" | x 2⅝" |
| Aida 18 | 4" | x 2" |
| Hardanger 22 | 3⅜" | x 1¾" |

# For Little Ones

*Our projects for little ones become Christmas classics with the sweet designs shown here. Whether stitched on bibs or other baby items, your precious little bundle will be outfitted in style.*

| X | DMC | ¼X | B'ST | COLOR |
|---|-----|-----|------|-------|
| | blanc | | | white |
| | 304 | | | dk red |
| R | 317 | | | grey |
| | 320 | | | green |
| | 321 | | | red |
| | 353 | | | peach |
| | 368 | | | lt green |
| | 413 | | | dk grey |
| | 434 | | | brown |
| | 435 | | | lt brown |
| | 436 | | | dk tan |
| | 437 | | | tan |
| | 500 | | | vy dk blue green |
| | 501 | | | dk blue green |

OUACHITA TECHNICAL COLLEGE

| X | DMC | ¼X | B'ST | COLOR |
|---|-----|-----|------|-------|
| □ | 502 | | | blue green |
| ☆ | 503 | ☐ | | lt blue green |
| ■ | 676 * | ◩ | ◪ | lt gold & gold metallic |
| ▨ | 722 | ◩ | | lt orange |
| ◉ | 725 | | | vy dk yellow |
| □ | 726 | ☐ | | dk yellow |
| ∷ | 727 | | | yellow |
| ○ | 738 | | | lt tan |
| ▨ | 739 | | | vy lt tan |
| ◇ | 754 | ◩ | | lt peach |
| A | 783 | ◩ | | topaz |
| C | 899 | | | pink |
| 2 | 928 | ◩ | | lt grey blue |
| 4 | 930 | | | dk blue grey |

| X | DMC | ¼X | B'ST | COLOR |
|---|-----|-----|------|-------|
| ✖ | 931 | ◩ | | blue grey |
| ★ | 932 | | | lt blue grey |
| − | 948 | ◩ | | lt flesh |
| ☆ | 3078 | | | lt yellow |
| ◇ | 3325 | ◩ | | lt blue |
| ■ | 3371 | | ◪ | brown black |
| ▨ | 3688 | ◩ | | mauve |
| E | 3689 | | | lt mauve |
| V | 3755 | ◩ | | blue |
| • | 3371 | | | brown black Fr. Knot |

\* Use 2 strands of lt gold and 1 strand
  of gold metallic.

Each design was stitched
over 14 mesh waste canvas
on purchased baby
garments (see Working on
Waste Canvas, pg. 142) or
prefinished items. Three
strands of floss were used
for Cross Stitch and 1 for
Backstitch and
French Knots.

*Designed by Lorraine
Birmingham.*

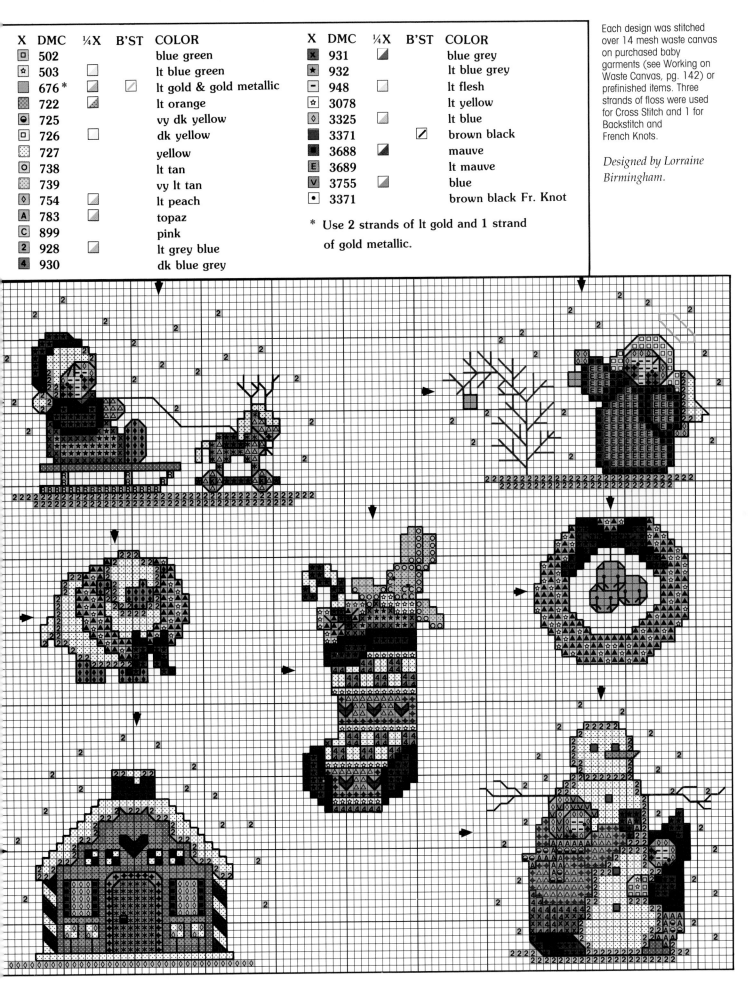

# Dashing Through the House

*Filling your home with the holiday spirit is easy with the wonderful projects in this collection. There are lots of designs for adorning fingertip towels, table linens, pot holders, and more, as well as custom-framed pieces that are sure to become Yuletide treasures. There's something for every decorating scheme, and no matter which design — or designs — you choose, each one works up in a jiffy so you can finish your other Christmas errands!*

# Santa Sampler

*The many faces of Santa Claus combine to make this adorable sampler that's sure to spread lots of Christmas cheer. The fun-loving gentlemen are also stitched individually on mini pillows.*

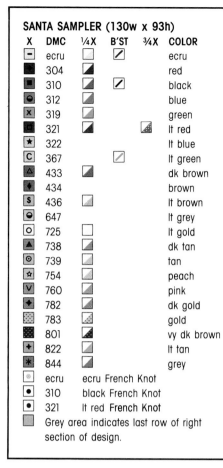

## SANTA SAMPLER (130w x 93h)

| X | DMC | ¼ X | B'ST | ¾ X | COLOR |
|---|-----|-----|------|-----|-------|
| − | ecru | | ✓ | | ecru |
| ■ | 304 | ◢ | | | red |
| ■ | 310 | ◢ | ✓ | | black |
| ◙ | 312 | ◢ | | | blue |
| ✕ | 319 | ◢ | | | green |
| ▦ | 321 | ◢ | | ◩ | lt red |
| ★ | 322 | ◢ | | | lt blue |
| C | 367 | | ✓ | | lt green |
| △ | 433 | ◢ | | | dk brown |
| ◆ | 434 | | | | brown |
| S | 436 | ◢ | | | lt brown |
| ◙ | 647 | | | | lt grey |
| ○ | 725 | | | | lt gold |
| ▲ | 738 | ◢ | | | dk tan |
| ◉ | 739 | ◢ | | | tan |
| ☆ | 754 | ◢ | | | peach |
| V | 760 | ◢ | | | pink |
| ◆ | 782 | ◢ | | | dk gold |
| ▒ | 783 | ▒ | | | gold |
| ▓ | 801 | ◢ | | | vy dk brown |
| ✦ | 822 | ◢ | | | lt tan |
| ✳ | 844 | ◢ | | | grey |
| ⊙ | ecru | | | | ecru French Knot |
| ● | 310 | | | | black French Knot |
| ● | 321 | | | | lt red French Knot |
| ▨ | | Grey area indicates last row of right section of design. | | | |

## SANTA SAMPLER (130w x 93h)

| | | | |
|---|---|---|---|
| 14 count | 9⅜" | x | 6¾" |
| 16 count | 8⅛" | x | 5⅞" |
| 18 count | 7¼" | x | 5¼" |
| 22 count | 6" | x | 4¼" |

**Santa Sampler** (shown on pages 74 and 75) was stitched on an 18" x 15" piece of Ivory Aida (14 ct). Three strands of floss were used for Cross Stitch and 1 for all other stitches. It was custom framed.

Each **Santa** (shown on pages 74 and 75) was stitched on Ivory Aida (14 ct). Three strands of floss were used for Cross Stitch and 1 for all other stitches. They were made into mini pillows.

    For each mini pillow, trim stitched piece 1" larger than design on all sides. Cut a piece of Ivory Aida the same size as stitched piece for backing. With wrong sides facing, use 1 strand of desired floss color and Running Stitches (see Stitch Diagrams, page 142) to join fabric pieces together ½" from bottom and side edges. Stuff with polyester fiberfill. Repeat to stitch across top of mini pillow ½" from edge. Fringe fabric to within one square of stitched lines.

*Designed by Kathie Rueger.*
*Needlework adaptation by Kathy Elrod.*

# Classic Table Linens

*Traditionally stitched in all one color, classic Nordic patterns embellish these festive table linens. They're a wonderful way to spread holiday cheer when lovingly placed about the house.*

# TABLE LINENS

**Note:** Table linens are stitched on Cracked Wheat Ragusa (14 ct) over 2 fabric threads, using 6 strands of floss for Cross Stitch.

**For a 13¾" x 36" table runner,** you will need one 15¾" x 36" piece of Cracked Wheat Ragusa (14 ct), embroidery floss (DMC 304 or Anc. 047), embroidery hoop (optional), and thread to match fabric.

1. With design centered and bottom of design 3" from one short edge of fabric, work design; repeat as necessary to within 1½" of each long edge. Repeat for remaining short edge.
2. Fold long edges of fabric ½" to wrong side; press. Fold ½" to wrong side again and hem. For fringe, machine stitch 2¼" from each short edge and pull threads up to machine-stitched lines.

**For a 10" x 18¾" bread cloth,** you will need one 12" x 18¾" piece of Cracked Wheat Ragusa (14 ct), embroidery floss (DMC 304 or Anc. 047), embroidery hoop (optional), and thread to match fabric.

1. Bread cloth design is between grey lines on chart. With design centered and bottom of design 1½" from one short edge of fabric, work design; repeat as necessary to within 1½" of each long edge.
2. To finish edges, follow step 2 of Table Runner instructions, machine stitching 1" from each short edge.

**For each 1¼" dia. napkin ring,** you will need one 4¾" x 7" piece of Cracked Wheat Ragusa (14 ct), embroidery floss (DMC 304 or Anc. 047), one 2" x 6" piece of buckram or lightweight cardboard, and thread to match fabric.

1. With napkin ring design centered between long edges of fabric and beginning ½" from left short edge, work design; repeat as necessary to within ½" of right short edge.
2. Center buckram on wrong side of stitched piece. Fold short edges of fabric over buckram; pin in place. Fold one long edge of fabric over buckram; pin in place. Fold remaining edge of fabric ¼" to wrong side; fold over buckram and pin in place. Whipstitch fabric in place; remove pins.
3. Whipstitch short edges together to form a ring.

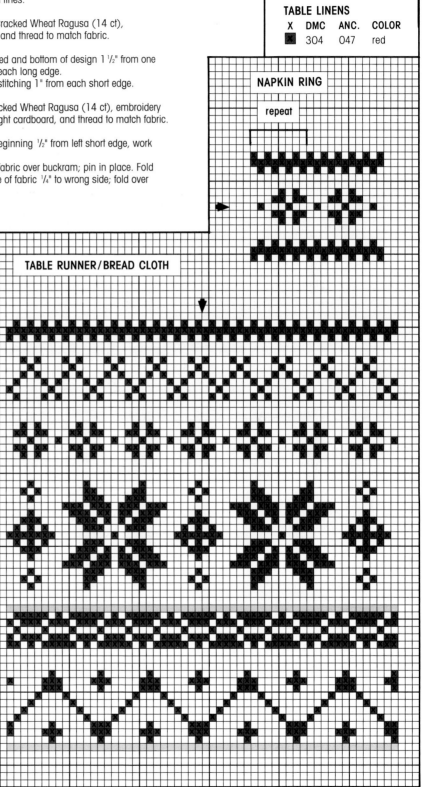

**TABLE LINENS**

| X | DMC | ANC. | COLOR |
|---|-----|------|-------|
| ■ | 304 | 047 | red |

**NAPKIN RING**

repeat

**TABLE RUNNER/BREAD CLOTH**

# A FRIENDLY SNOWMAN

*Stitched on a heart-shaped door pillow, this friendly snowman and his companions will greet holiday visitors with merry Christmas wishes.*

## SNOWMAN AND FRIENDS (50w x 52h)

| X | DMC | ¼X | B'ST | COLOR | X | DMC | ¼X | B'ST | COLOR |
|---|-----|-----|------|-------|---|-----|-----|------|-------|
| ▫ | blanc | ▫ | | white | ★ | 498 | ◢ | | dk red |
| − | ecru | ◣ | | ecru | △ | 721 | ◢ | | orange |
| ■ | 310 | | ◿ | black | ▦ | 801 | ◢ | | brown |
| ▨ | 321 | ◣ | | red | ▫ | 822 | ▫ | | beige |
| 2 | 434 | | | lt brown | N | 909 | ◣ | | green |
| ▨ | 435 | ◢ | | tan | + | 911 | ◣ | | lt green |
| O | 436 | ◣ | | lt tan | • | 310 | | | black French Knot |

**Snowman and Friends:** Stitched over 2 fabric threads on an 11" square of Tea-Dyed Irish Linen (28 ct). Two strands of floss were used for Cross Stitch and 1 for all other stitches. Made into a door pillow.

For door pillow, fold a piece of tracing paper in half. Place folded edge of paper along dashed line of Heart pattern, page 143, and trace pattern onto tracing paper; leaving tracing paper folded, cut out pattern. Unfold pattern and press to flatten. Referring to photo for placement, pin pattern to wrong side of stitched piece. Use a fabric marking pencil to draw around pattern. Cut out stitched piece. Repeat to cut lining piece from tan fabric and backing piece from Tea-Dyed Irish Linen. With wrong sides facing and matching raw edges, baste stitched piece and lining together close to raw edges.

For handle, press long edges of a 2" x 10" strip of Tea-Dyed Irish Linen ¼" to center; repeat, pressing ³/₈" of long edges to center. Whipstitch edges together at center. With right sides facing and matching raw edges, baste each end of handle to stitched piece at top of heart close to raw edges.

With right sides facing and leaving an opening for turning, use a ¹/₄" seam allowance to sew pillow backing to pillow top; clip seam allowance. Turn pillow right side out, carefully pushing edges outward. Stuff pillow with polyester fiberfill and sew final closure by hand. Refer to photo and use 6 strands of DMC 321 floss to work Running Stitch (**Fig. 10**, page 142), on front of pillow approx. ¹/₄" from seam.

*Designed by Michele Arzaga for Family Line, Inc. ©1983*

# Gingerbread Greeting

*With fresh-baked goodness, this little gingerbread boy offers warm Christmas greetings. Stitched on a pot holder, he'll add a festive touch to your kitchen.*

**GINGERBREAD BOY (40w x 42h)**

| X | DMC | B'ST | JPC | COLOR |
|---|---|---|---|---|
| ▦ | blanc | | 1001 | white |
| ★ | 319 | | 6246 | green |
| ■ | 321 | | 3500 | red |
| V | 367 | | 6018 | lt green |
| X | 434 | | 5000 | brown |
| – | 436 | | 5943 | lt brown |
| 3 | 762 | | 8510 | grey |
| ■ | 3371 | ╱ | 5478 | brown black |
| 8 | 3712 | | | lt red |

**Gingerbread Boy:** Stitched on the Aida (14 ct) insert of an ecru pot holder. Three strands of floss used for Cross Stitch and 1 for Backstitch.

*Designed by Lorraine Birmingham.*

# Happy Holiday Towels

*Stitched on hand towels, these familiar symbols of the season are gleeful reminders of Yuletide fun. The festive fingertips make cheery Christmas accents for the bath or kitchen, and they're great thank-you gifts for a holiday hostess, too.*

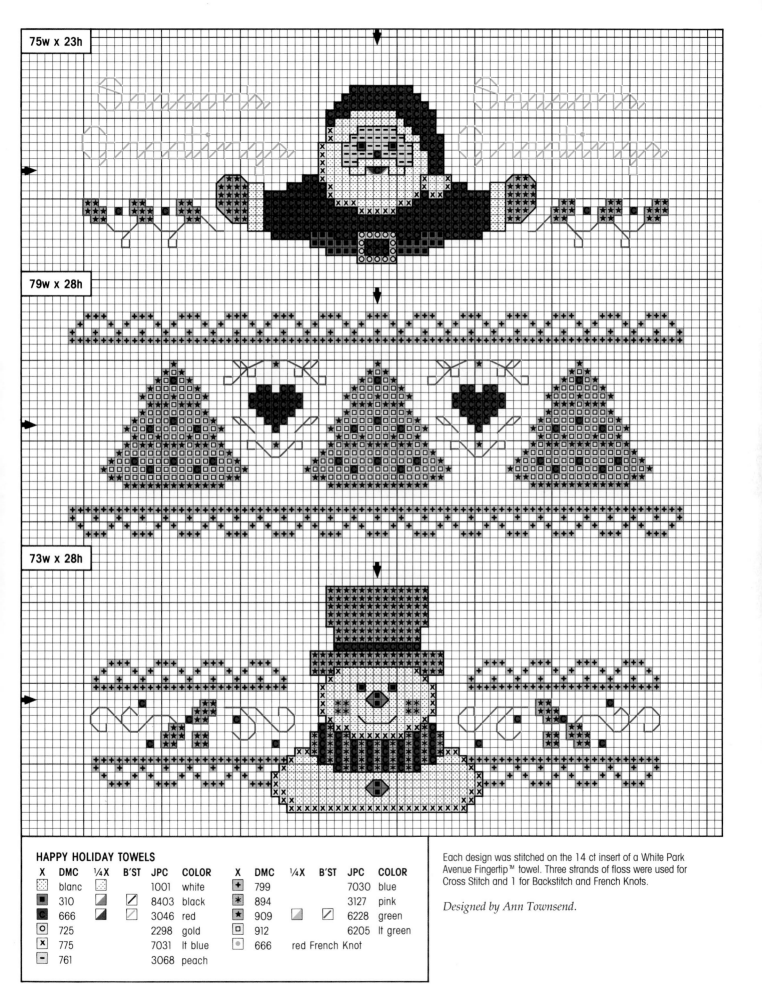

## HAPPY HOLIDAY TOWELS

| X | DMC | 1/4X | B'ST | JPC | COLOR | X | DMC | 1/4X | B'ST | JPC | COLOR |
|---|---|---|---|---|---|---|---|---|---|---|---|
| | blanc | | | 1001 | white | + | 799 | | | 7030 | blue |
| ■ | 310 | | / | 8403 | black | * | 894 | | | 3127 | pink |
| C | 666 | | / | 3046 | red | ★ | 909 | | / | 6228 | green |
| O | 725 | | | 2298 | gold | □ | 912 | | | 6205 | lt green |
| X | 775 | | | 7031 | lt blue | • | 666 | | | | red French Knot |
| – | 761 | | | 3068 | peach | | | | | | |

Each design was stitched on the 14 ct insert of a White Park Avenue Fingertip™ towel. Three strands of floss were used for Cross Stitch and 1 for Backstitch and French Knots.

*Designed by Ann Townsend.*

# A
# Basketful
# of
# Greetings

*This Christmas, why not let your favorite teddies welcome your friends with a merry cross-stitched message!*

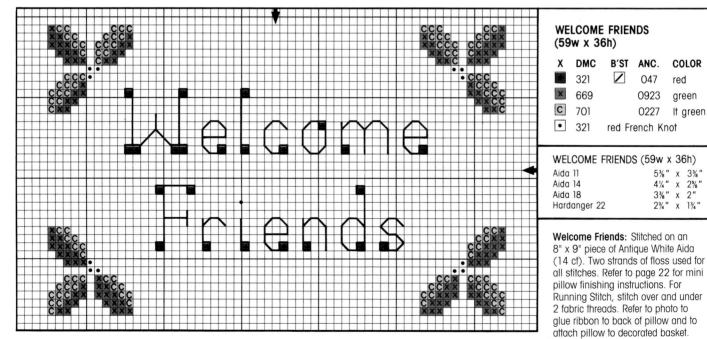

**WELCOME FRIENDS (59w x 36h)**

| X | DMC | B'ST | ANC. | COLOR |
|---|-----|------|------|-------|
| ■ | 321 | ╱ | 047 | red |
| ✕ | 669 | | 0923 | green |
| C | 701 | | 0227 | lt green |
| • | 321 | | | red French Knot |

**WELCOME FRIENDS (59w x 36h)**

| | | | |
|---|---|---|---|
| Aida 11 | 5⅜" | x | 3⅜" |
| Aida 14 | 4¼" | x | 2⅝" |
| Aida 18 | 3⅜" | x | 2" |
| Hardanger 22 | 2¾" | x | 1¾" |

**Welcome Friends:** Stitched on an 8" x 9" piece of Antique White Aida (14 ct). Two strands of floss used for all stitches. Refer to page 22 for mini pillow finishing instructions. For Running Stitch, stitch over and under 2 fabric threads. Refer to photo to glue ribbon to back of pillow and to attach pillow to decorated basket.

# "I Believe" Stocking

*Proclaiming a childlike trust in Santa Claus, the sweet message on the cuff of this candy-striped stocking is certain to warm your heart.*

**"I BELIEVE" STOCKING (85 x 31)**

| X | DMC | B'ST | JPC | COLOR |
|---|-----|------|-----|-------|
| ★ | 321 | | 3500 | red |
| O | 726 | | 294 | yellow |
| | 890 | ╱ | 6021 | dk green |
| △ | 909 | | 6228 | green |

**"I BELIEVE" STOCKING (85w x 31h)**

| | |
|---|---|
| Aida 11 | 7³/₄" x 2⁷/₈" |
| Aida 14 | 6¹/₈" x 2¹/₄" |
| Aida 18 | 4³/₄" x 1³/₄" |
| Hardanger 22 | 3⁷/₈" x 1¹/₂" |

**I Believe** was stitched on a 4 ¹/₄" x 17" piece of White Aida (14 ct) using 2 strands of floss for Cross Stitch and 1 for Backstitch. See Stocking Finishing, pg. 143.

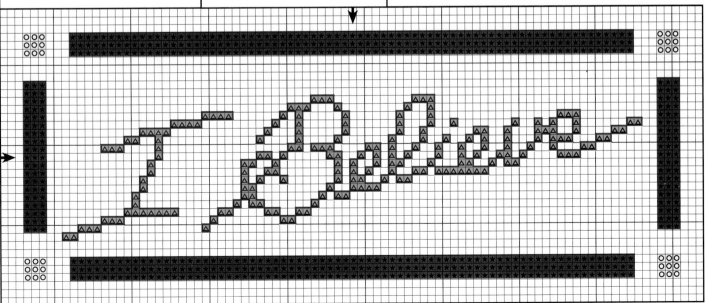

# Little Old Santas

*Bearing gifts for all who've been good, this troupe of miniature Santas is ready to spread cheer and goodwill to everyone. Stitched on an Anne Cloth afghan and also fashioned into fringed mini pillow ornaments, these designs are sure to become favorites!*

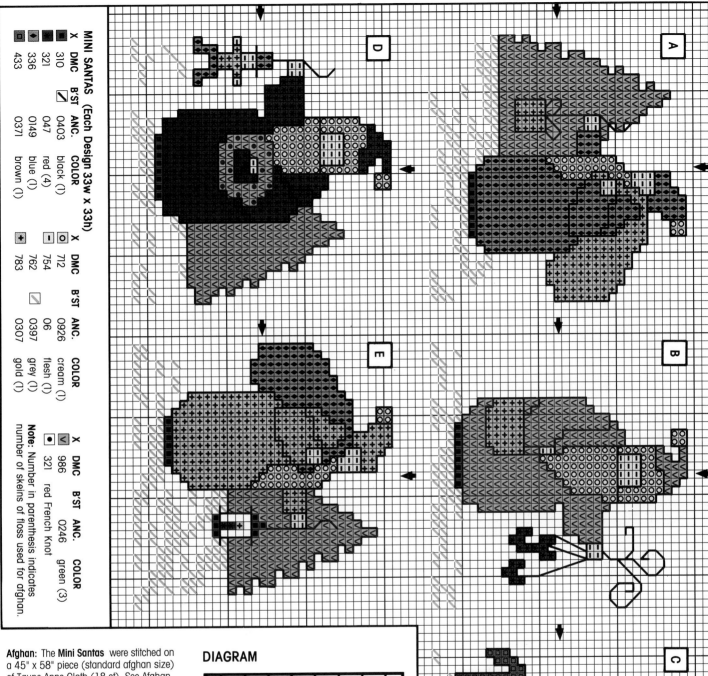

## MINI SANTAS (Each Design 33w x 33h)

| X | B'ST | DMC | ANC. | COLOR |
|---|------|-----|------|-------|
| | | 310 | 0403 | black (1) |
| | | 321 | 047 | red (4) |
| | | 336 | 0149 | blue (1) |
| | | 433 | 0371 | brown (1) |

| X | B'ST | DMC | ANC. | COLOR |
|---|------|-----|------|-------|
| | | 712 | 0926 | cream (1) |
| | | 754 | 06 | flesh (1) |
| | | 762 | 0397 | grey (1) |
| | | 783 | 0307 | gold (1) |

| X | B'ST | DMC | ANC. | COLOR |
|---|------|-----|------|-------|
| | | 986 | 0246 | green (3) |
| | | 321 | | red French Knot |

**Note:** Number in parenthesis indicates number of skeins of floss used for afghan.

**Afghan:** The **Mini Santas** were stitched on a 45" x 58" piece (standard afghan size) of Taupe Anne Cloth (18 ct). See Afghan Finishing, pg. 143.

Refer to Diagram for placement of designs on fabric. Stitch over 2 fabric threads, using 6 strands of floss for Cross Stitch, 2 for Backstitch, and 2 for French Knots. (**Note:** Designs on afghan were stitched using red for all Santa coats and hats.)

**Mini Pillows:** Each of the designs was stitched on a 7" square of Dirty Aida (14 ct). Two strands of floss were used for Cross Stitch, 1 for Backstitch, and 1 for French Knots. Refer to page 18 for finishing instructions.

*Designed by Julia Bailey of The Spinning Wheel.*

## DIAGRAM

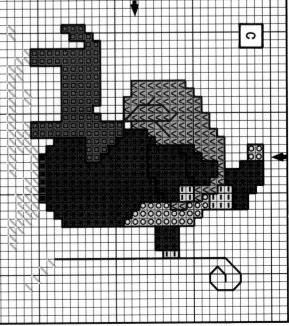

# Gentle Nativity

*With loving simplicity, this little Nativity sends a message
sweet and clear — tuck away a bit of Christmas warmth
and gentleness to keep with you throughout the year.
Reminding us of that blessed event so long ago, this
touching design is appropriate for any season.*

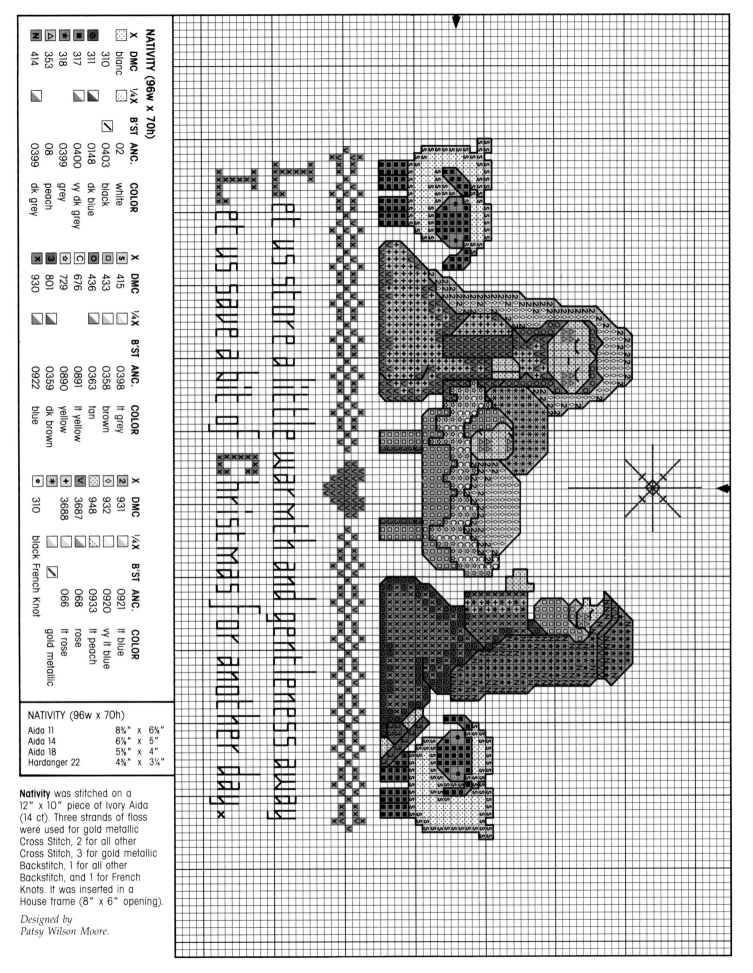

**NATIVITY (96w x 70h)**

| X | ¼X | B'ST | DMC | ANC. | COLOR |
|---|----|------|-----|------|-------|
| | | | blanc | 02 | white |
| | | | 310 | 0403 | black |
| | | ◢ | 311 | 0148 | dk blue |
| | | | 317 | 0400 | vy dk blue |
| | | | 318 | 0399 | grey |
| | | | 353 | 08 | peach |
| | | | 414 | 0399 | dk grey |

| X | ¼X | B'ST | DMC | ANC. | COLOR |
|---|----|------|-----|------|-------|
| S | | | 415 | 0398 | lt grey |
| | | | 433 | 0358 | brown |
| | | | 436 | 0363 | tan |
| C | | | 676 | 0891 | lt yellow |
| O | | | 729 | 0890 | yellow |
| | | | 801 | 0359 | dk brown |
| | | | 930 | 0922 | blue |

| X | ¼X | B'ST | DMC | ANC. | COLOR |
|---|----|------|-----|------|-------|
| ● | | | 931 | 0921 | lt blue |
| ✳ | | | 932 | 0920 | vy lt blue |
| + | | | 948 | 0933 | lt peach |
| V | | | 3687 | 068 | rose |
| ◇ | | | 3688 | 066 | lt rose |
| 2 | | | | | gold metallic |
| | | ◢ | 310 | | black French Knot |

**NATIVITY (96w x 70h)**

| | |
|---|---|
| Aida 11 | 8¾" x 6⅜" |
| Aida 14 | 6⅞" x 5" |
| Aida 18 | 5⅜" x 4" |
| Hardanger 22 | 4⅜" x 3¼" |

**Nativity** was stitched on a 12" x 10" piece of Ivory Aida (14 ct). Three strands of floss were used for gold metallic Cross Stitch, 2 for all other Cross Stitch, 3 for gold metallic Backstitch, 1 for all other Backstitch, and 1 for French Knots. It was inserted in a House frame (8" x 6" opening).

*Designed by Patsy Wilson Moore.*

# A Cheery Tray

*Accenting a handy tray, our winsome little Christmas cub
will help you serve up the holiday spirit. The cheery design has
a sprinkling of metallic threads to add sparkle to the occasion.*

## TREE CHEERS (94w x 70h)

| | | | | |
|---|---|---|---|---|
| 14 count | 6¾" | x | 5" | |
| 16 count | 5⅞" | x | 4⅜" | |
| 18 count | 5¼" | x | 4" | |
| 22 count | 4⅜" | x | 3¼" | |

## TREE CHEERS (94w x 70h)

| X | DMC | ¼X | B'ST | JPC | COLOR | X | DMC | ¼X | B'ST | JPC | COLOR |
|---|---|---|---|---|---|---|---|---|---|---|---|
| | blanc | | | 1001 | white | | 498 | | | 3410 | dk red |
| | *blanc | | | 1001 | white | | 666 | | | 3046 | lt red |
| | 310 | ◤ | ╱ | 8403 | black | | 676 | | | 2874 | lt gold |
| | 312 | | | 7979 | dk blue | | 729 | | | 2875 | gold |
| | † 318 | | | 8511 | grey | | 762 | | | 8510 | vy lt grey |
| | 321 | | ╱ | 3500 | red | | 815 | | | 3000 | vy dk red |
| | 334 | | | 7977 | blue | | 890 | ◤ | | 6021 | dk green |
| | 367 | ◤ | | 6018 | green | | 898 | ◤ | | 5476 | vy dk brown |
| | † 414 | | | 8513 | dk grey | | *928 | | | 7225 | blue grey |
| | 415 | | | 8398 | lt grey | | 3348 | | ◻ | 6266 | lt green |
| | † 415 | | | 8398 | lt grey | | 3755 | | | | lt blue |
| | 433 | ◤ | | 5471 | dk brown | | | | | | |
| | 434 | | | 5000 | brown | | | | | | |
| | 436 | | | 5943 | lt brown | | | | | | |
| | 437 | | ◻ | 5942 | vy lt brown | | | | | | |

\* Use 3 strands of floss and 1 strand of Kreinik Blending Filament - 032.

† Use 3 strands of floss and 1 strand of Kreinik Blending Filament - 001HL.

**Tree Cheers** was stitched on a 16" x 14" piece of Antique White Lugana (25 ct). The design was stitched over 2 fabric threads. Three strands of floss were used for Cross Stitch, 2 for red Backstitch, and 1 for all other Backstitch. It was inserted in a purchased tray (10" x 7" opening).

*Original artwork by Vicky Howard.*
*Needlework adaptation by Jane Chandler.*

# PETITE SAMPLER

*Create remembrances of yesteryear with this miniature Christmas sampler. Stitched in rich holiday colors, the petite design is filled with tiny Yuletide motifs and old-fashioned charm.*

**Sampler** was stitched on a 6" x 7" piece of Ivory Aida (18 ct). Two strands of floss were used for Cross Stitch, 1 for Backstitch, and 1 for French Knots. It was inserted into a purchased frame. For chart of numerals, see page 143.

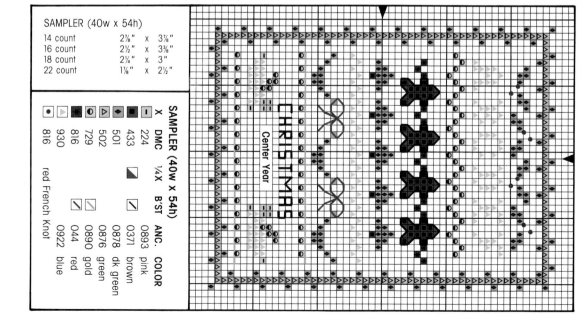

SAMPLER (40w x 54h)

| 14 count | 2⅞" | x | 3⅞" |
|---|---|---|---|
| 16 count | 2½" | x | 3⅜" |
| 18 count | 2¼" | x | 3" |
| 22 count | 1⅞" | x | 2½" |

| X | 1/4X | B'ST | DMC | ANC. | COLOR |
|---|---|---|---|---|---|
| | | | 224 | 0893 | pink |
| | ◪ | ◹ | 433 | 0371 | brown |
| | | ◹ | 501 | 0878 | dk green |
| | ◹ | | 502 | 0876 | green |
| | | | 729 | 0890 | gold |
| | | | 816 | 044 | red |
| | | | 930 | 0922 | blue |
| | | | 816 | | red French Knot |

# Holiday Towels

*This pair of fingertip towels, adorned with our lovely poinsettia and horn designs, will add a bright holiday touch to your bath.*

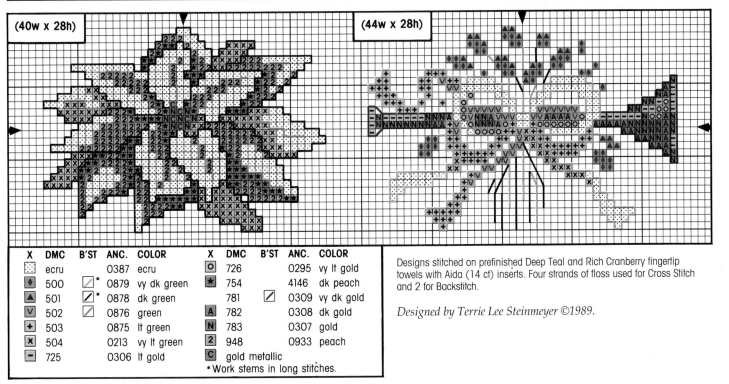

(40w x 28h)

(44w x 28h)

| X | DMC | B'ST | ANC. | COLOR |
|---|-----|------|------|-------|
| ▦ | ecru | | 0387 | ecru |
| ◆ | 500 | ╱* | 0879 | vy dk green |
| ▲ | 501 | ╱* | 0878 | dk green |
| V | 502 | ╱ | 0876 | green |
| + | 503 | | 0875 | lt green |
| X | 504 | | 0213 | vy lt green |
| − | 725 | | 0306 | lt gold |

| X | DMC | B'ST | ANC. | COLOR |
|---|-----|------|------|-------|
| O | 726 | | 0295 | vy lt gold |
| ★ | 754 | | 4146 | dk peach |
| | 781 | ╱ | 0309 | vy dk gold |
| A | 782 | | 0308 | dk gold |
| N | 783 | | 0307 | gold |
| 2 | 948 | | 0933 | peach |
| C | gold metallic | | | |

*Work stems in long stitches.

Designs stitched on prefinished Deep Teal and Rich Cranberry fingertip towels with Aida (14 ct) inserts. Four strands of floss used for Cross Stitch and 2 for Backstitch.

*Designed by Terrie Lee Steinmeyer ©1989.*

# Quaint Sampling

*Perfect for stocking stuffers, these quick-to-stitch gifts feature quaint holiday designs that were inspired by antique samplers.*

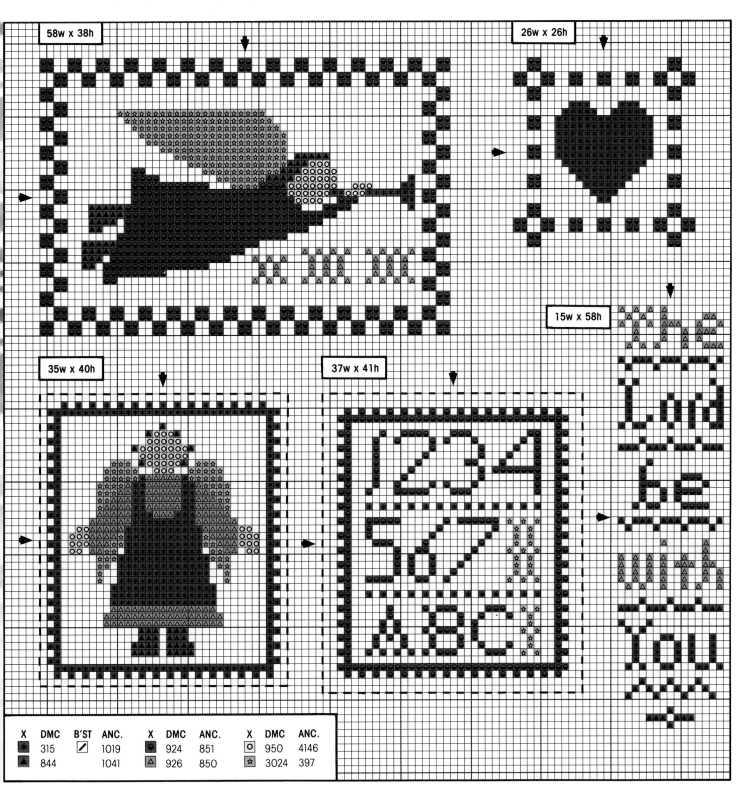

| X | DMC | B'ST | ANC. | X | DMC | ANC. | X | DMC | ANC. |
|---|-----|------|------|---|-----|------|---|-----|------|
| ✳ | 315 | ✎ | 1019 | ◐ | 924 | 851 | ○ | 950 | 4146 |
| ▲ | 844 | | 1041 | △ | 926 | 850 | ★ | 3024 | 397 |

Each design was stitched on Raw Belfast Linen (32 ct) over 2 fabric threads. Two strands of floss were used for all stitches. The ABC design was custom framed.

## Bookmark Finishing
Trim stitched piece to desired size plus ¹/₂" on all sides for fringe. Machine stitch ¹/₂" from raw edges; fringe fabric to one fabric thread from machine-stitched lines.

## Pincushion/Sachet Finishing
Trim stitched piece to desired size plus ¹/₂" on all sides. Cut backing fabric (same fabric as stitched piece) same size as stitched piece. Matching right sides and raw edges, use a ¹/₂" seam allowance to machine stitch fabric pieces together, leaving an opening at bottom edge. Trim corner seam allowances diagonally. Turn pincushion/sachet right side out, carefully pushing corners outward; stuff with polyester fiberfill. For sachet, place a few drops of scented oil on a small amount of fiberfill and insert in middle of sachet. Sew final closure by hand.

## Pillow With Cording Finishing
For pillow top, trim stitched piece to desired size plus ¹/₂" on all sides. Cut pillow backing same size as stitched piece. To make cording, cut a bias strip of fabric 2"w and outer dimension of pillow top plus 1". Lay purchased cord along center of strip on wrong side of fabric; fold strip over cord. Use zipper foot to machine baste along length of strip close to cord. Starting at bottom edge of pillow top and 1" from end of cording, baste cording to right side of pillow top with finished edge toward center of pillow and raw edges facing outward. Opening ends of cording, cut cord to fit exactly. Insert one end of cording in the other; turn top end under ¹/₂" and baste in place. Use zipper foot to sew cording in place along seam line. Matching right sides and raw edges, use zipper foot to sew pillow top to pillow backing along seam line, leaving an opening at bottom edge. Clip seam allowances at corners. Turn pillow right side out, carefully pushing corners outward. Stuff pillow with polyester fiberfill; sew final closure by hand.

*Designed by Kandace Thomas.*

# Christmas Cuffs

*Hanging from the mantel or along the banister, our elegant velvet stockings will make beautiful holiday accents. With their Irish linen cuffs and handsome Yuletide designs, these classic beauties are sure to become cherished keepsakes!*

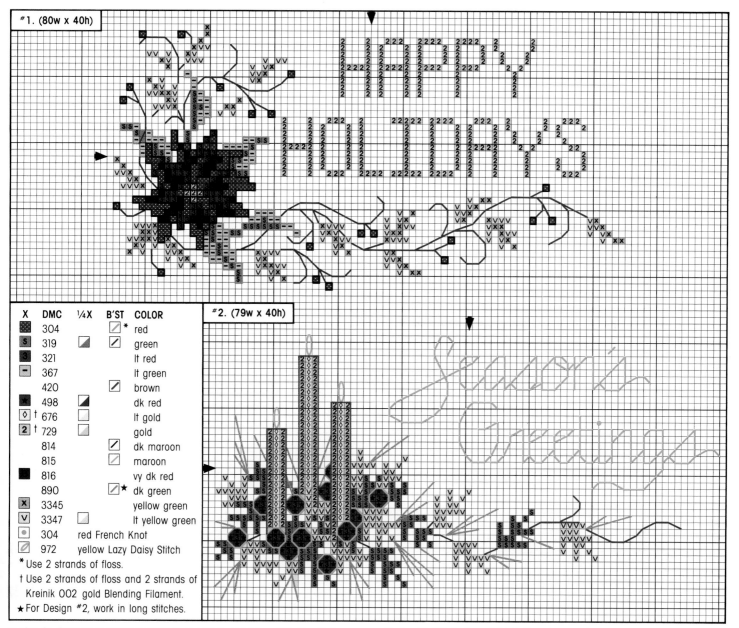

**#1.** (80w x 40h)

**#2.** (79w x 40h)

| X | DMC | ¼X | B'ST | COLOR |
|---|---|---|---|---|
| ▨ | 304 | | ◻ * | red |
| s | 319 | ◹ | ◻ | green |
| 3 | 321 | | | lt red |
| − | 367 | | | lt green |
| | 420 | | ◹ | brown |
| ★ | 498 | ◤ | | dk red |
| ◇ † | 676 | | ◻ | lt gold |
| 2 † | 729 | | ◻ | gold |
| | 814 | | ◹ | dk maroon |
| | 815 | | ◻ | maroon |
| ■ | 816 | | | vy dk red |
| | 890 | | ◹ ★ | dk green |
| x | 3345 | | | yellow green |
| v | 3347 | ◻ | | lt yellow green |
| • | 304 | | | red French Knot |
| ◹ | 972 | | | yellow Lazy Daisy Stitch |

\* Use 2 strands of floss.

† Use 2 strands of floss and 2 strands of Kreinik 002 gold Blending Filament.

★ For Design #2, work in long stitches.

**Design #1:** Stitched over 2 fabric threads on a White Irish Linen (28 ct) cuff of a Green Velvet Christmas Stocking. Three strands of floss used for Cross Stitch (unless otherwise indicated in color key) and 1 for Backstitch.

**Design #2:** Stitched over 2 fabric threads on a White Irish Linen (28 ct) cuff of a Red Velvet Christmas Stocking. Three strands of floss used for Cross Stitch, 1 for Backstitch (unless otherwise indicated in color key), 2 for French Knots, and 1 for Lazy Daisy Stitches.

*Designed by Jane Chandler.*

# Holiday Chickadee

*With fluttering wings and chipper antics, the black-capped chickadee
livens up a winter day. As he alights among the branches of a brightly
hued holly bush, this tiny feathered friend makes our hearts sing.
What a welcome visitor on a snowy morning!*

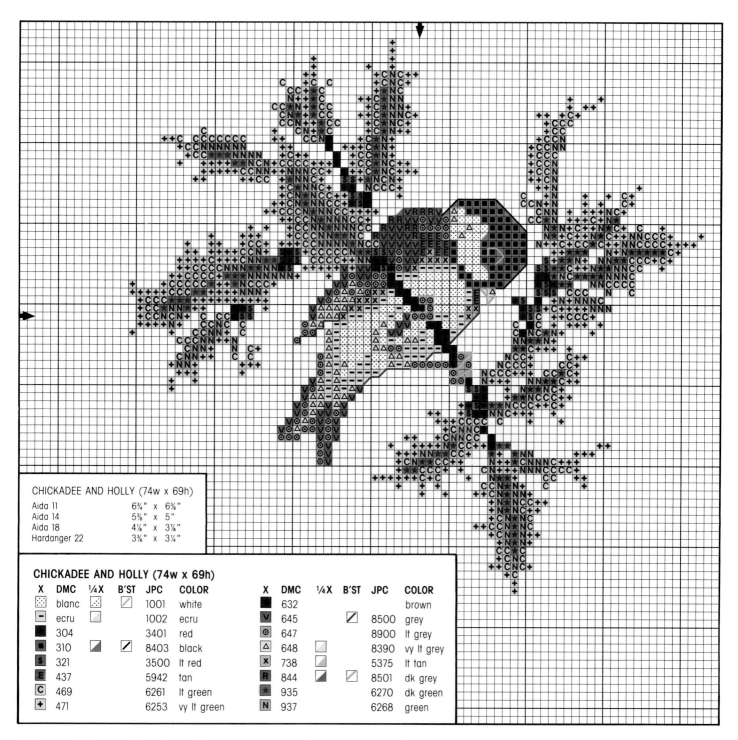

**CHICKADEE AND HOLLY (74w x 69h)**

| Aida 11 | 6¾" x 6⅜" |
|---|---|
| Aida 14 | 5⅜" x 5" |
| Aida 18 | 4⅛" x 3⅞" |
| Hardanger 22 | 3⅜" x 3¼" |

**CHICKADEE AND HOLLY (74w x 69h)**

| X | DMC | ¼X | B'ST | JPC | COLOR | X | DMC | ¼X | B'ST | JPC | COLOR |
|---|---|---|---|---|---|---|---|---|---|---|---|
| | blanc | | | 1001 | white | | 632 | | | | brown |
| - | ecru | | | 1002 | ecru | V | 645 | | | 8500 | grey |
| | 304 | | | 3401 | red | ⊙ | 647 | | | 8900 | lt grey |
| | 310 | | | 8403 | black | △ | 648 | | | 8390 | vy lt grey |
| S | 321 | | | 3500 | lt red | X | 738 | | | 5375 | lt tan |
| E | 437 | | | 5942 | tan | R | 844 | | | 8501 | dk grey |
| C | 469 | | | 6261 | lt green | ★ | 935 | | | 6270 | dk green |
| + | 471 | | | 6253 | vy lt green | N | 937 | | | 6268 | green |

**Chickadee and Holly** was stitched on a 13" square of Cream Belfast Linen (32 ct). The design was stitched over 2 fabric threads. Two strands of floss were used for Cross Stitch and 1 for Backstitch. It was made into a pillow.

For pillow, cut stitched piece 2" larger than design on all sides. Cut one piece of coordinating fabric same size as stitched piece for backing.

For cording, cut one 35" x 2½" bias strip (pieced as necessary) of coordinating fabric. Lay purchased cord along center of strip on wrong side of fabric; fold strip over cord, matching raw edges. Using zipper foot, baste along length of strip close to cord; trim seam allowance to ½". Matching raw edges and beginning at bottom center, pin cording to right side of stitched piece. Ends of cording should overlap approximately 2"; pin overlapping end out of way.

Starting 2" from beginning end of cording,

baste cording to stitched piece. Clip seam allowance of cording at corners. On overlapping end of cording, remove 2½" of basting; fold end of fabric back and trim cord so that it meets beginning end of cord. Fold end of fabric under ½"; wrap fabric over beginning end of cording, Finish basting cording to stitched piece.

For fabric and lace ruffle, cut a 62" x 5" strip of coordinating fabric (pieced as necessary) and a 62" length of 1½"w flat lace trim. Fold short ends of fabric strip ½" to wrong side; fold strip in half lengthwise with wrong sides together and press. Fold short ends of lace trim ½" to wrong side and press. Matching raw edge of ruffle and edge of lace, baste layers together close to raw edge. Gather fabric strip and lace trim to fit stitched piece.

Matching raw edges and beginning at one edge of stitched piece, use a ½" seam allowance to

sew fabric and lace ruffle to right side of stitched piece.

With right sides facing and leaving an opening for turning, use a zipper foot to sew stitched piece and backing fabric together using a ½" seam allowance; clip seam allowance at corners. Turn pillow right side out, carefully pushing corners outward. Stuff pillow with polyester fiberfill and sew final closure by hand.

*Designed by Holly Chérie Barbo.*

# Sleepy Santa

*After his whirlwind trip around the world each Christmas Eve, Santa happily slips into his nightshirt and heads for bed. As children everywhere are awakening to discover their Christmas treasures, he's enjoying the sweet dreams that come from doing good deeds.*

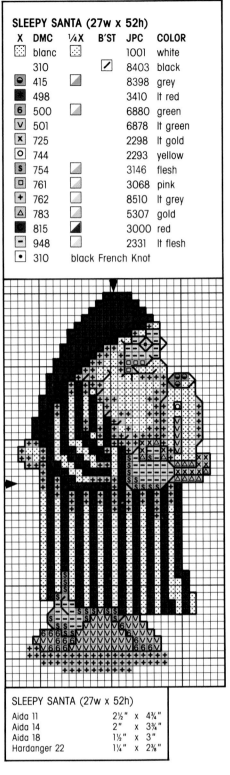

## SLEEPY SANTA (27w x 52h)

| X | DMC | ¼X | B'ST | JPC | COLOR |
|---|-----|-----|------|-----|-------|
| ⊡ | blanc | ⊡ | | 1001 | white |
| | 310 | | ◸ | 8403 | black |
| ⊟ | 415 | | ◸ | 8398 | grey |
| ✳ | 498 | | | 3410 | lt red |
| 6 | 500 | | ◸ | 6880 | green |
| V | 501 | | | 6878 | lt green |
| X | 725 | | | 2298 | lt gold |
| O | 744 | | | 2293 | yellow |
| S | 754 | | ◸ | 3146 | flesh |
| ▫ | 761 | | ◸ | 3068 | pink |
| + | 762 | | ◸ | 8510 | lt grey |
| △ | 783 | | ◸ | 5307 | gold |
| ◼ | 815 | | ◿ | 3000 | red |
| - | 948 | | ◸ | 2331 | lt flesh |
| ⊙ | 310 | | black French Knot | | |

## SLEEPY SANTA (27w x 52h)

| | | | |
|---|---|---|---|
| Aida 11 | 2½" | x | 4¾" |
| Aida 14 | 2" | x | 3¾" |
| Aida 18 | 1½" | x | 3" |
| Hardanger 22 | 1¼" | x | 2⅜" |

**Sleepy Santa** was stitched on a 6" x 8" piece of Ivory Aida (18 ct). Two strands of floss were used for Cross Stitch and 1 for all other stitches. It was inserted in a candle screen frame (2 ½" x 3 ½" opening).

*Designed by Claudia Rohling.*

# Pretty Towels

*Pulled thread stitches lend old-fashioned flair to colorful hand towels for the holidays. For an attractive gift basket, present a pair of the pretty towels along with some fancy soaps.*

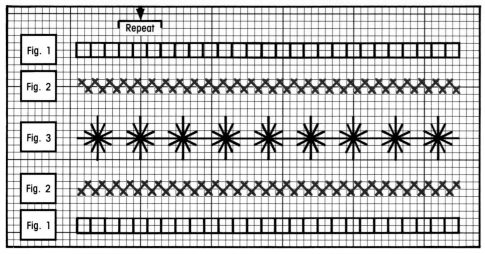

The design was stitched on a prefinished fingertip towel (14 ct) using desired colors of embroidery floss. (**Note:** Refer to chart and **Figs. 1**, **2**, and **3** to work designs.) With design centered between long edges of insert, use 2 strands of floss to work design across entire insert, repeating as necessary.

**FOUR-SIDED STITCH**
Fig. 1

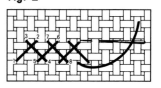

**HERRINGBONE STITCH**
Fig. 2

**DIAMOND EYELET STITCH**
Fig. 3

# Love & Joy

*Bring love and joy to your holiday celebration with this simple sampler. Accented with Christmasy motifs, the design is quick and easy to stitch for yourself or for a gift.*

**LOVE AND JOY (85w x 93h)**

| X | DMC | ANC. | COLOR |
|---|-----|------|-------|
| ■ | 500 | 683 | dk green |
| ◎ | 501 | 878 | green |
| ✚ | 680 | 901 | gold |

| X | DMC | ANC. | COLOR |
|---|-----|------|-------|
| ■ | 902 | 897 | red |
| ■ | 924 | 851 | blue |

**LOVE AND JOY (85w x 93h)**

| | | | |
|---|---|---|---|
| 14 count | 6⅛" | x | 6¾" |
| 16 count | 5⅜" | x | 5⅞" |
| 18 count | 4¾" | x | 5¼" |
| 22 count | 3⅞" | x | 4¼" |

**Love and Joy** was stitched on a 10" x 12" piece of Natural Irish Linen (32 ct). The design was stitched over 2 fabric threads. Two strands of floss were used for Cross Stitch. It was custom framed.

*Designed by Cecilia Turner.*

# Holly-Day Table Set

*When your holiday dining calls for decorative table settings, reach for this distinctive set that features napkins, a bread cloth, and place mats. A tiny holly border and holiday alphabet let you embellish each with seasonal style.*

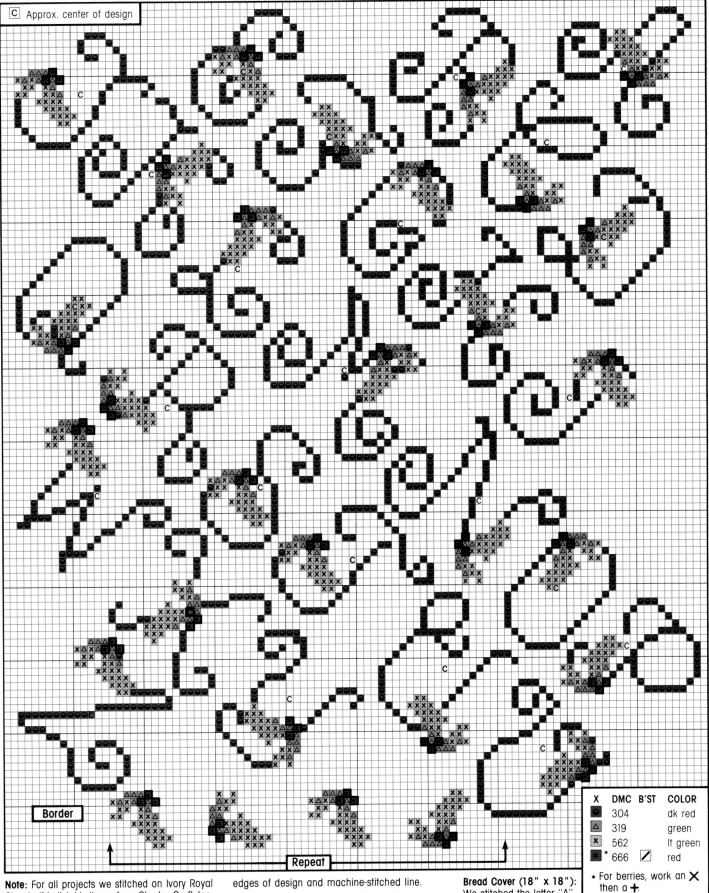

C Approx. center of design

Border

Repeat

| X | DMC | B'ST | COLOR |
|---|-----|------|-------|
| ● | 304 | | dk red |
| △ | 319 | | green |
| ✕ | 562 | | lt green |
| ✱ | 666 * | ╱ | red |

* For berries, work an ✕ then a ✚

**Note:** For all projects we stitched on Ivory Royal Classic (14 ct) table linens from Charles Craft, Inc. We used 2 strands of floss for Cross Stitch and 1 for Backstitch.

**Napkin (15" x 15"):** We stitched the letter "A" in one corner of the napkin, leaving ¾" between

edges of design and machine-stitched line.

**Placemat (18" x 13"):** We stitched the border design along both short edges of the placemat, beginning and ending 1" from machine-stitched line on long edges. We left ¾" between bottom of design and machine-stitched line on short edges.

**Bread Cover (18" x 18"):** We stitched the letter "A" from the alphabet in one corner of the bread cover, leaving ¾" between edges of design and machine-stitched line.

*Alphabet by Linda Calhoun.*

# Smart Little Bear

*"Bearing" his soul, this little guy will surely inspire others to believe in Santa! Stitched on a pot holder, he'll win a place in your heart as well.*

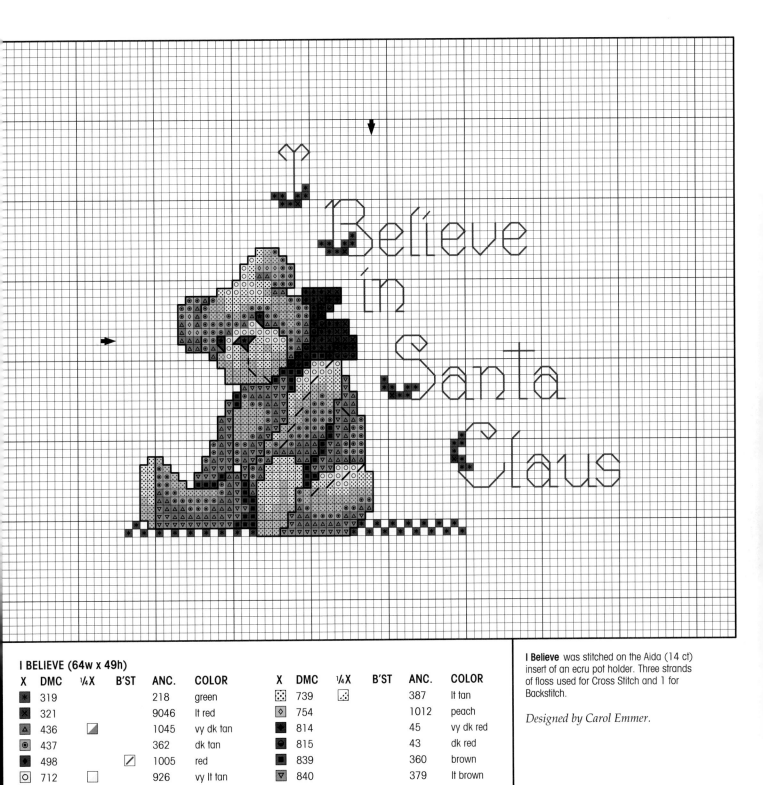

**I BELIEVE (64w x 49h)**

| X | DMC | ¼X | B'ST | ANC. | COLOR | | X | DMC | ¼X | B'ST | ANC. | COLOR |
|---|-----|-----|------|------|-------|---|---|-----|-----|------|------|-------|
| ✴ | 319 | | | 218 | green | | ▦ | 739 | ⬚ | | 387 | lt tan |
| ✖ | 321 | | | 9046 | lt red | | ◇ | 754 | | | 1012 | peach |
| △ | 436 | ◿ | | 1045 | vy dk tan | | ◆ | 814 | | | 45 | vy dk red |
| ◉ | 437 | | | 362 | dk tan | | ⬡ | 815 | | | 43 | dk red |
| ◆ | 498 | | ◿ | 1005 | red | | ■ | 839 | | | 360 | brown |
| ○ | 712 | ☐ | | 926 | vy lt tan | | ▽ | 840 | | | 379 | lt brown |
| ▦ | 738 | ◪ | | 361 | tan | | ✴ | 3021 | ◿ | ◿ | 905 | grey brown |

**I Believe** was stitched on the Aida (14 ct) insert of an ecru pot holder. Three strands of floss used for Cross Stitch and 1 for Backstitch.

*Designed by Carol Emmer.*

# Cheery Stocking

*Beribboned holly and blossoms are regally finished with a festive message in elegant script. A quilted stocking of Yuletide paisley provides the perfect background for this beautiful design.*

## CHRISTMAS STOCKING (88w x 50h)

| X | DMC | 1/4X | B'ST | ANC. | COLOR |
|---|---|---|---|---|---|
| ▓ | blanc | ▨ | | 2 | white |
| ▓ | 310 | ◪ | ☑ | 403 | black |
| ◆ | 500 | ◪ | | 683 | vy dk green |
| ▓ | 561 | ◪ | | 212 | dk green |
| ✱ | 562 | ◪ | | 210 | green |
| ◻ | 564 | ◻ | | 206 | vy lt green |
| ◆ | 642 | ◪ | | 392 | beige |
| V | 644 | ◪ | | 830 | lt beige |
| ▓ | 666 | ◪ | | 46 | lt red |
| − | 676 | | | 891 | gold |
| ◆ | 677 | | | 886 | lt gold |
| ★ | 680 | | | 901 | dk gold |
| ▓ | 815 | ◪ | | 43 | dk red |
| ◆ | 817 | ◪ | | 13 | red |
| ▨ | 822 | ▨ | | 390 | vy lt beige |
| ◉ | 893 | ◪ | | 28 | pink |
| | 902 | | ☑ | 897 | vy dk red |
| ▨ | 913 | ▨ | | 204 | lt green |
| | 934 | | ☑ | 862 | avocado |
| | 3790 | | ☑ | 393 | dk beige |
| | Kreinik 002 - Fine Braid | | ☑ | | |
| ◉ | Kreinik 002 - Fine Braid French Knot | | | | |

The design was stitched on the White Aida (14 ct) cuff of a prefinished stocking. Three strands of floss were used for Cross Stitch and 1 for Backstitch and French Knots.

*Design by Donna Vermillion Giampa.*

# A Sweet Noel

*Nestled among evergreen branches in our Noel basket, a cheerful gingerbread couple will charm visitors with their holiday forecast. What a sweet welcoming committee for your front door or entryway!*

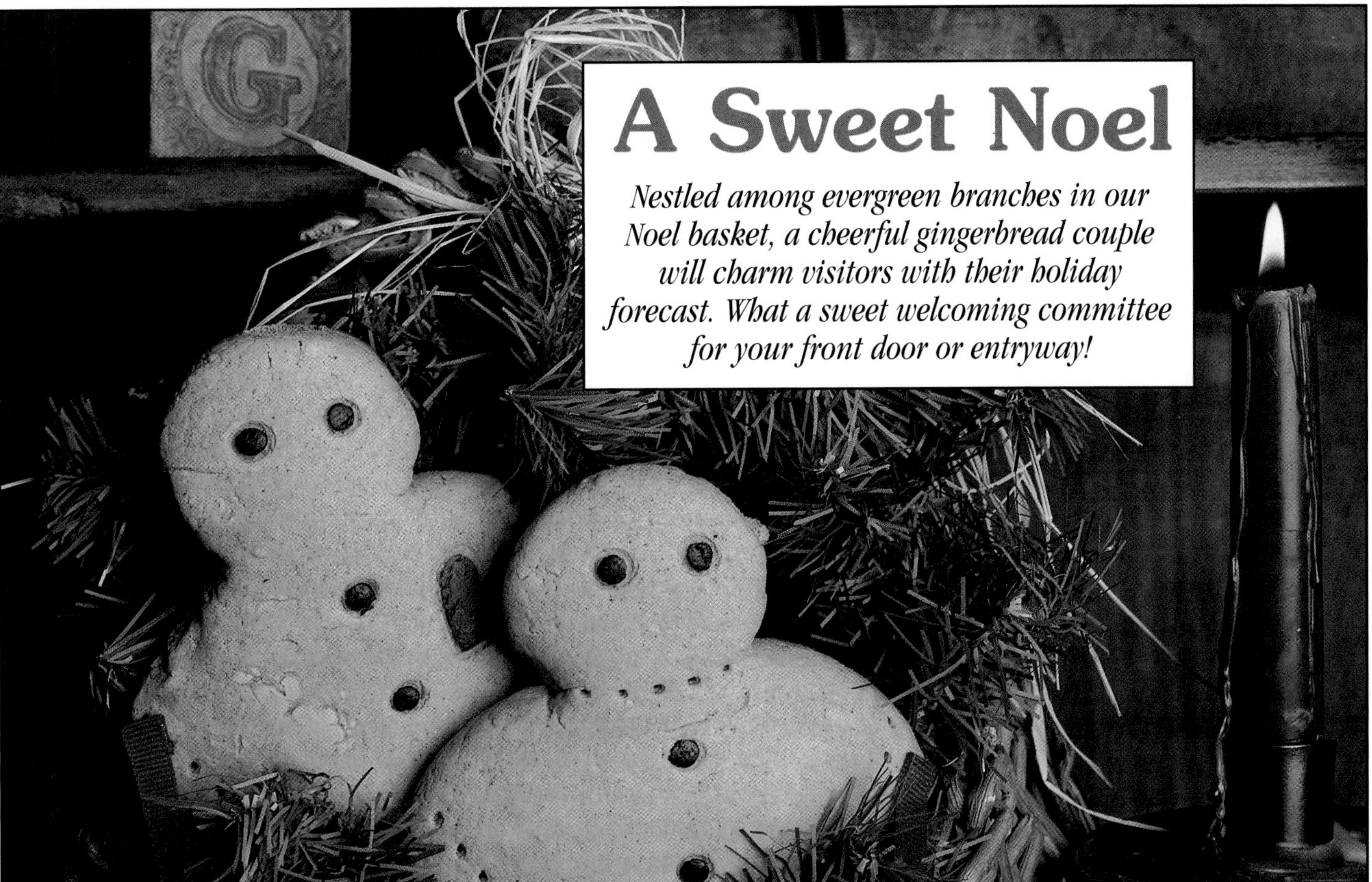


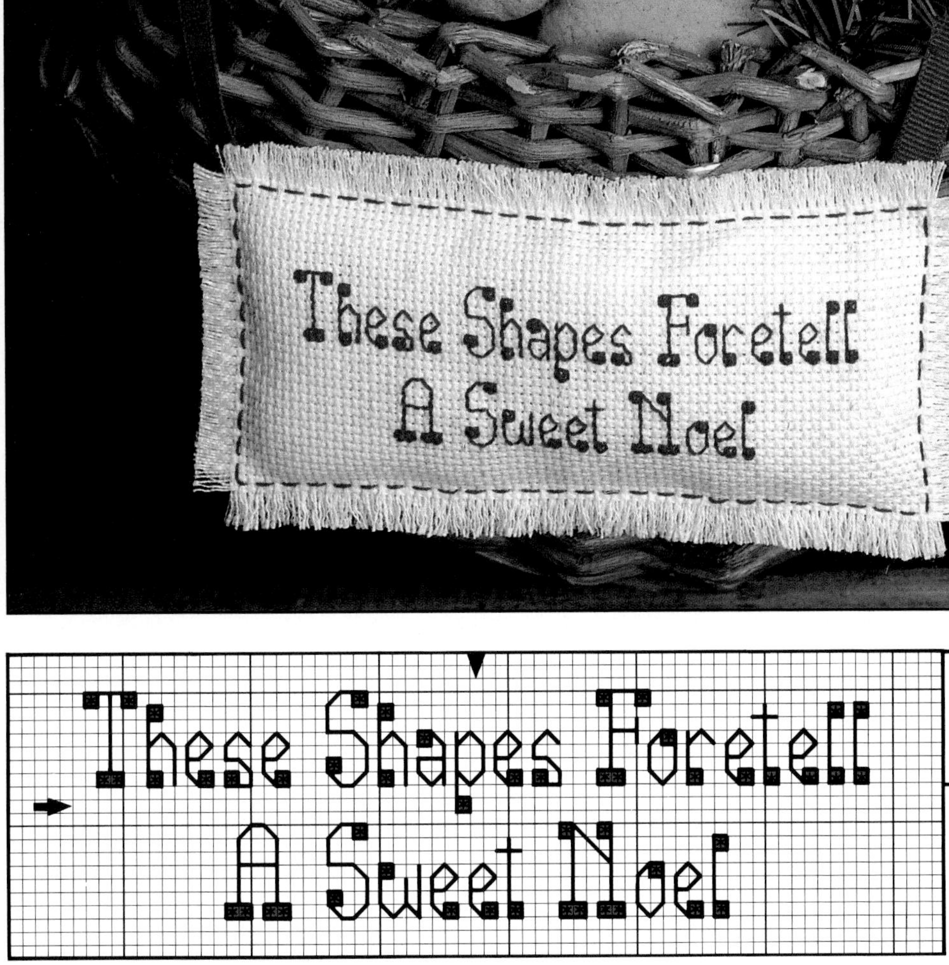


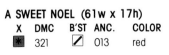

**A SWEET NOEL (61w x 17h)**

| X | DMC | B'ST | ANC. | COLOR |
|---|---|---|---|---|
| ■ | 321 | ⁄ | 013 | red |

**A Sweet Noel:** Stitched on a 7" x 10" piece of Fiddler's Lite (14 ct). Two strands of floss used for all stitches. Made into a mini pillow and attached to a decorated wall basket. Refer to page 22 for finishing instructions. For Running Stitch, stitch over 2 fabric threads and under 1 fabric thread.

# Country Fingertips

*The homey charm of country plaids inspired these festive fingertip towels. They're guaranteed to bring a bit of holiday cheer to your Christmas.*

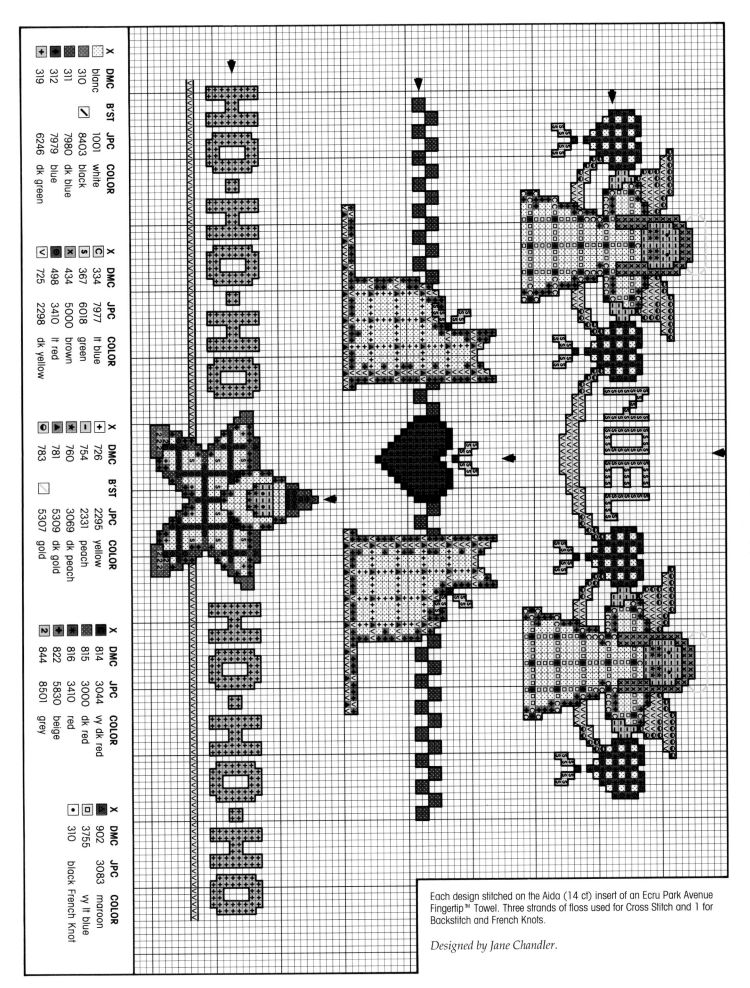

| X | | | | DMC | JPC | COLOR |
|---|---|---|---|---|---|---|
| + | ● | ▓ | ░ | | | |
| | | | | blanc | 1001 | white |
| | | | | 310 | 8403 | black |
| | | | | 311 | 7980 | dk blue |
| | | | | 312 | 7979 | blue |
| | | | | 319 | 6246 | dk green |

B'ST ☑

| X | | | | DMC | JPC | COLOR |
|---|---|---|---|---|---|---|
| ☑ | ● | ✕ | ░ | | | |
| | C | S | | 334 | 7977 | lt blue |
| | | | | 367 | 6018 | green |
| | | | | 434 | 5000 | brown |
| | | | | 498 | 3410 | lt red |
| | | | | 725 | 2298 | dk yellow |

| X | | | | DMC | JPC | COLOR |
|---|---|---|---|---|---|---|
| ◐ | ▶ | ★ | | | | |
| | | | + | 726 | 2295 | yellow |
| | | | | 754 | 2331 | peach |
| | | | | 760 | 3069 | dk peach |
| | | | | 781 | 5309 | dk gold |
| | | | | 783 | 5307 | gold |

B'ST ᒣᒣᒣ

| X | | | | DMC | JPC | COLOR |
|---|---|---|---|---|---|---|
| ☑ | ◆ | ✱ | ■ | | | |
| | | | | 814 | 3044 | vy dk red |
| | | | | 815 | 3000 | dk red |
| | | | | 816 | 3410 | red |
| | | | | 822 | 5830 | beige |
| | | | | 844 | 8501 | grey |

| X | | DMC | JPC | COLOR |
|---|---|---|---|---|
| ● | ▣ | | | |
| | | 902 | 3083 | maroon |
| | | 3755 | | vy lt blue |
| | | 310 | | black French Knot |

Each design stitched on the Aida (14 ct) insert of an Ecru Park Avenue Fingertip™ Towel. Three strands of floss used for Cross Stitch and 1 for Backstitch and French Knots.

*Designed by Jane Chandler.*

# Blessed Christmas

*Remembering the true reason for the season is easy with this lovely portrait of Mary and Baby Jesus. The classic image is sure to become a cherished holiday heirloom for generations to come.*

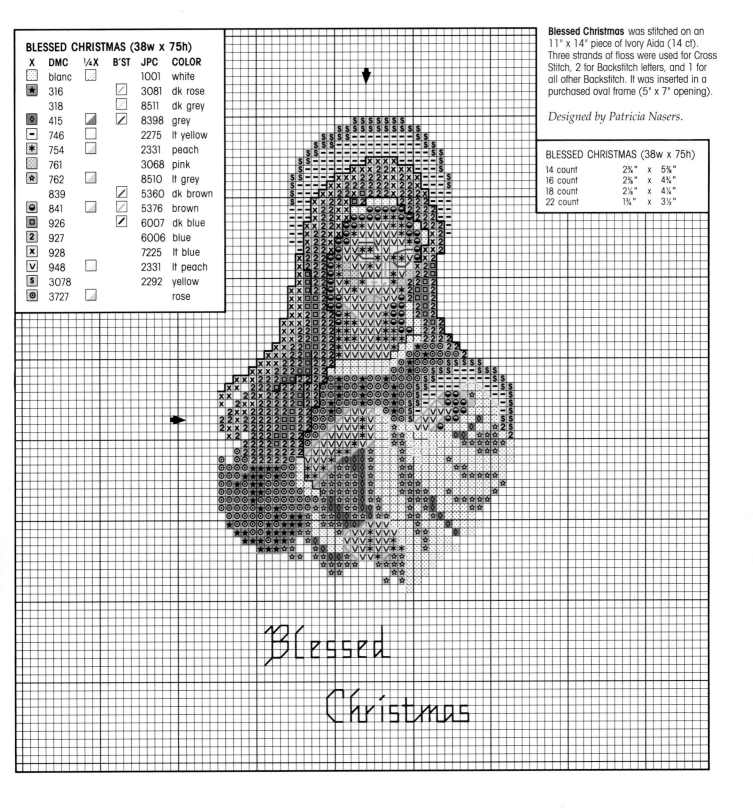

**BLESSED CHRISTMAS (38w x 75h)**

| X | DMC | ¼X | B'ST | JPC | COLOR |
|---|-----|-----|------|-----|-------|
| ⬚ | blanc | ⬚ | | 1001 | white |
| ★ | 316 | | ◿ | 3081 | dk rose |
| | 318 | | ◿ | 8511 | dk grey |
| ◆ | 415 | ◣ | ◿ | 8398 | grey |
| − | 746 | ▢ | | 2275 | lt yellow |
| ✳ | 754 | ◣ | | 2331 | peach |
| ▒ | 761 | | | 3068 | pink |
| ☆ | 762 | ◣ | | 8510 | lt grey |
| | 839 | | ◿ | 5360 | dk brown |
| ◖ | 841 | ◣ | ◿ | 5376 | brown |
| ▢ | 926 | | ◿ | 6007 | dk blue |
| 2 | 927 | | | 6006 | blue |
| X | 928 | | | 7225 | lt blue |
| V | 948 | ▢ | | 2331 | lt peach |
| S | 3078 | | | 2292 | yellow |
| ◉ | 3727 | ▢ | | | rose |

**Blessed Christmas** was stitched on an 11" x 14" piece of Ivory Aida (14 ct). Three strands of floss were used for Cross Stitch, 2 for Backstitch letters, and 1 for all other Backstitch. It was inserted in a purchased oval frame (5" x 7" opening).

*Designed by Patricia Nasers.*

**BLESSED CHRISTMAS (38w x 75h)**

| | | | |
|---|---|---|---|
| 14 count | 2¾" | x | 5⅜" |
| 16 count | 2⅜" | x | 4¾" |
| 18 count | 2⅛" | x | 4¼" |
| 22 count | 1¾" | x | 3½" |

# Heavenly Pillow

*Joyful angels bearing sweet tidings make this pillow an irresistible accent for your home. The heavenly design will brighten up any room for the holidays.*

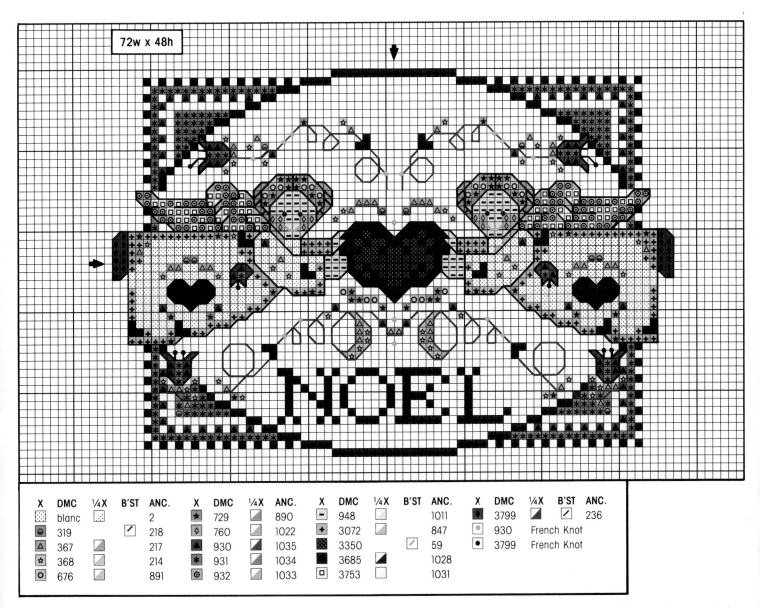

**72w x 48h**

| X | DMC | ¼X | B'ST | ANC. | X | DMC | ¼X | ANC. | X | DMC | ¼X | ANC. | X | DMC | ¼X | ANC. | X | DMC | ¼X | B'ST | ANC. |
|---|---|---|---|---|---|---|---|---|---|---|---|---|---|---|---|---|---|---|---|---|---|
| | blanc | | | 2 | ★ | 729 | | 890 | − | 948 | | 1011 | | 3799 | | ✓ | 236 |
| ⊖ | 319 | | ✓ | 218 | ◇ | 760 | | 1022 | ✚ | 3072 | | 847 | ⊙ | 930 | | French Knot |
| △ | 367 | | | 217 | ▲ | 930 | | 1035 | ▦ | 3350 | | | ✓ | 59 | ● | 3799 | | French Knot |
| ★ | 368 | | | 214 | ✳ | 931 | | 1034 | ■ | 3685 | | 1028 | | | |
| ◎ | 676 | | | 891 | ⊙ | 932 | | 1033 | ▢ | 3753 | | 1031 | | | |

Design was stitched on a 14" x 12" piece of Antique White Lugana (25 ct) over 2 fabric threads. Three strands of floss were used for Cross Stitch and 1 for all other stitches. Made into a pillow.

**Pillow Finishing**
**Step 1.** For pillow top, trim stitched piece to desired size plus ½" on all sides. Cut backing fabric same size as stitched piece.

**Step 2.** To make cording, cut a bias strip of fabric 2"w and outer dimension of pillow top plus 1". (**Note:** This strip may be pieced if necessary.) Lay purchased cord along center of strip on wrong side of fabric; fold strip over cord. Use zipper foot to machine baste along length of strip close to cord.

To make ruffle, cut a strip of fabric twice desired finished width plus 1" for seam allowances and twice outer dimension of pillow top (measure edges of pillow top; then double measurement). (**Note:** This strip may be pieced if necessary.) Press short ends ½" to wrong side. Fold strip in half lengthwise with wrong sides together and press. Baste close to raw edge. Make another basting seam ¼" from the first. Pull basting threads, drawing up gathers to fit pillow top.

**Step 3.** For cording, start at bottom edge of pillow top and 1" from end of cording. Baste cording to right side of pillow top with finished edge toward center of pillow and raw edges facing outward. Opening ends of cording, cut cord to fit exactly. Insert one end of cording in the other; turn top end under ½" and baste in place. Use zipper foot to sew cording in place along seam line.

For ruffle, start at bottom edge of pillow top and use zipper foot to sew ruffle to right side of pillow top along seam line with finished edge toward center of pillow and raw edges facing outward. Join ends of ruffle using blind stitches.

**Step 4.** Matching right sides and raw edges, use zipper foot to sew pillow top to pillow backing along seam line, leaving an opening at bottom edge. Trim corner seam allowances diagonally. Turn pillow right side out, carefully pushing corners outward. Stuff pillow with polyester fiberfill; sew final closure by hand.

*Designed by Diane Brakefield.*

# Jiffy Little Gifts

When you present a friend with something handmade, you're truly giving a gift from the heart. Just a few stitches are all it takes to create a token that lets someone know how truly special he or she is to you. With that sentiment in mind, we assembled this unique collection of quick handcrafted Christmas gifts. You'll find wonderful ideas for all the people in your life, including neighbors, teachers, and family members. There are even designs to adorn store-bought packages, too. You can't go wrong with our festive projects!

# A Homemade Christmas

*The merry motifs from our pot holder also add charm to projects such as a jar lid, a mini pillow, and gift tags. They'll lend a touch of home to your holiday food gifts.*

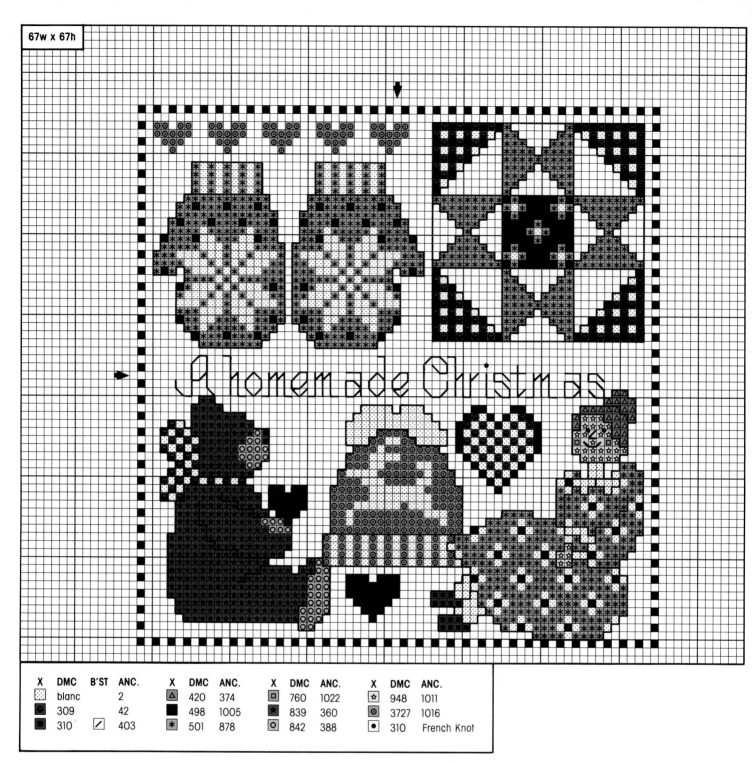

**67w x 67h**

A homemade Christmas

| X | DMC | B'ST | ANC. | X | DMC | ANC. | X | DMC | ANC. | X | DMC | ANC. | X | DMC | ANC. |
|---|---|---|---|---|---|---|---|---|---|---|---|---|---|---|---|
| | blanc | | 2 | △ | 420 | 374 | □ | 760 | 1022 | ★ | 948 | 1011 | | | |
| | 309 | | 42 | | 498 | 1005 | ✳ | 839 | 360 | ◎ | 3727 | 1016 | | | |
| | 310 | ╱ | 403 | ✳ | 501 | 878 | ○ | 842 | 388 | ● | 310 | French Knot | | | |

**Gift Tag:** Bear was stitched on a 5" square of Natural Perforated Paper (14 ct). Three strands of floss were used for Cross Stitch and 1 for Backstitch. Trim to within one square of design.

**Jar Lid:** Quilt was stitched on an 8" square of Ivory Aida (14 ct). Three strands of floss were used for Cross Stitch and 1 for Backstitch. Inserted in a wide mouth jar lid.

**Mini Pillow:** Cap, hearts, and doll were stitched on a 9" x 8½" piece of Ivory Aida (14 ct). Three strands of floss were used for Cross Stitch and 1 for all other stitches. For mini pillow, trim stitched piece to desired size plus ½" on all sides. Cut backing fabric (same fabric as stitched piece) same size as stitched piece. Matching wrong sides and raw edges, machine stitch fabric pieces together ½" from bottom and side edges. Stuff pillow with polyester fiberfill; machine stitch across top of pillow ½" from edges. Fringe fabric to one square from machine-stitched lines.

**Package Ornaments:** Mittens were stitched separately on 4½" squares Natural Perforated Paper (14 ct). Three strands of floss were used for C Stitch and 1 for Backstitch. Trim to within one square of design.

**Pot Holder:** Design was stitched on the Ivory Aida (14 ct) insert of a prefinished pot holder. Three strands of floss were used for Cross Stitch and 1 for all other stitches.

*Designed by Polly Carbonari.*

# Heartwarming Jar Lids

*Celebrate the season with the sweet tastes of Christmas! Just right for gift-giving, jars topped with these festive designs will help you say "Happy Holidays" in an extra-special way.*

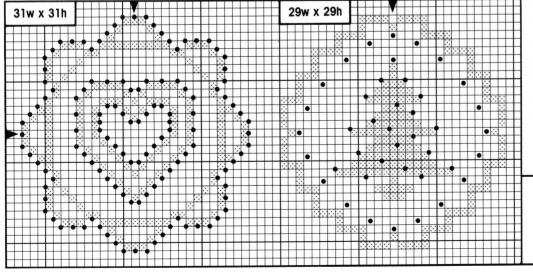

**31w x 31h**

**29w x 29h**

The heart design was stitched on a 7" square of Red Aida (14 ct). The tree design was stitched on a 7" square of Emerald Green Aida (14 ct). Two strands of floss were used for Cross Stitch and 2 for French Knots. They were inserted into wide mouth plastic jar lids (see Jar Lid Finishing, page 143).

*Designed by Sallie Lloyd.*

| **CHRISTMAS JAR LIDS** | | | |
|---|---|---|---|
| **X** | **DMC** | **JPC** | **COLOR** |
| ▨ | blanc | 1001 | white |
| ⊡ | white French Knot | | |

# Santa's Alphabet

*Christmas always spells fun, and our festive alphabet gives you free rein to dress up a basket, linens, clothing, and more! Candy canes, Santas, and greenery add a touch of color to our Yuletide letters.*

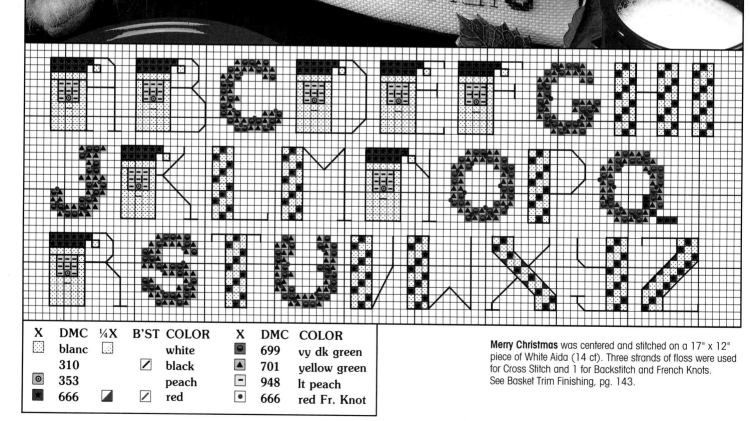

| X | DMC | ¼X | B'ST | COLOR | X | DMC | COLOR |
|---|---|---|---|---|---|---|---|
| | blanc | | | white | ◉ | 699 | vy dk green |
| | 310 | | ✓ | black | ▲ | 701 | yellow green |
| ◉ | 353 | | | peach | – | 948 | lt peach |
| ★ | 666 | ◣ | ✓ | red | ⊙ | 666 | red Fr. Knot |

**Merry Christmas** was centered and stitched on a 17" x 12" piece of White Aida (14 ct). Three strands of floss were used for Cross Stitch and 1 for Backstitch and French Knots. See Basket Trim Finishing, pg. 143.

# Cheerful Basket Cloths

*Stitched on basket cloths, our cute borders will add a dash of Christmas cheer to holiday goodies.*

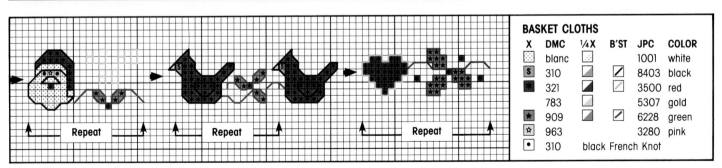

## BASKET CLOTHS

| X | DMC | ¼X | B'ST | JPC | COLOR |
|---|-----|-----|------|-----|-------|
| ▒ | blanc | ▫ | | 1001 | white |
| S | 310 | ◤ | ◺ | 8403 | black |
| ✱ | 321 | ◤ | ◺ | 3500 | red |
| | 783 | ◲ | | 5307 | gold |
| ★ | 909 | ◤ | ◺ | 6228 | green |
| ☆ | 963 | | | 3280 | pink |
| • | 310 | | black French Knot | | |

Each design stitched and repeated across each side of a White Soft Touch™ (14 ct) Breadcover with bottom of design 7 fabric threads from machine-stitched line. Three strands of floss used for Cross Stitch and 1 for all other stitches. To finish corners of basket cloth, cut a 3" square out of each corner. Machine stitch ½" from raw edges; clip inner corners diagonally to machine-stitched lines. Fringe fabric to machine-stitched lines.

*Designed by Ann Townsend.*

# Season's Greetings Mugs

*Lots of fun to stitch for quick gifts or as treats for yourself, these colorful holiday mugs are bursting with Christmas cheer.*

**64w x 40h**

**42w x 42h**

**39w x 39h**

NOEL

**74w x 33h**

| X | DMC | B'ST | ANC. | X | DMC | B'ST | ANC. |
|---|-----|------|------|---|-----|------|------|
| | blanc | | 2 | ★ | 754 | | 1012 |
| | 310 | / | 403 | − | 775 | | 128 |
| ★ | 321 | / | 9046 | | 909 | | 923 |
| ★ | 436 | | 1045 | | 911 | | 205 |
| | 666 | | 46 | | 321 | French Knot | |
| ◇ | 725 | | 305 | | 909 | French Knot | |

Each design was stitched on a 10¼" x 3½" piece of Vinyl-Weave™ (14 ct). Three strands of floss were used for Cross Stitch, 2 for 321 and 909 Backstitch and French Knots, and 1 for 310 Backstitch. Inserted in a Stitch-A-Mug™.

Place design on Vinyl-Weave™ 1" from desired short edge. (**Note:** Stitch design on right end of vinyl if mug is to used by a right-handed person and on left end of vinyl for a left-handed person.) Place Vinyl-Weave™ in mug with short edges of vinyl aligned with handle. Remove stitched piece before washing mug.

*Designed by Ann Townsend.*

123

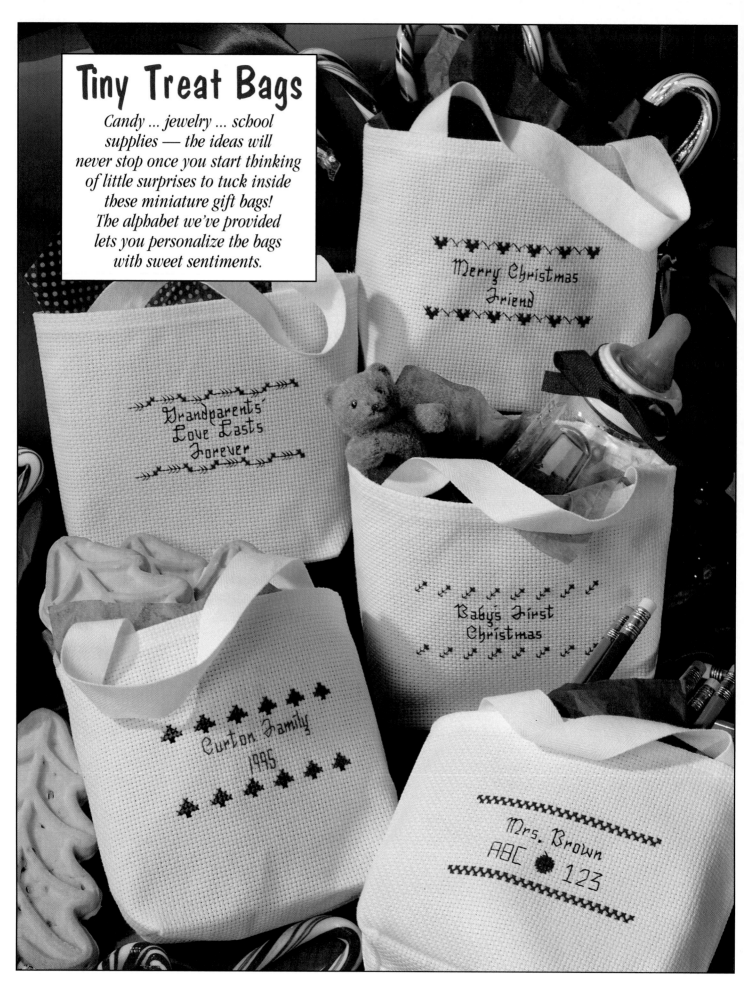

# Tiny Treat Bags

*Candy ... jewelry ... school supplies — the ideas will never stop once you start thinking of little surprises to tuck inside these miniature gift bags! The alphabet we've provided lets you personalize the bags with sweet sentiments.*

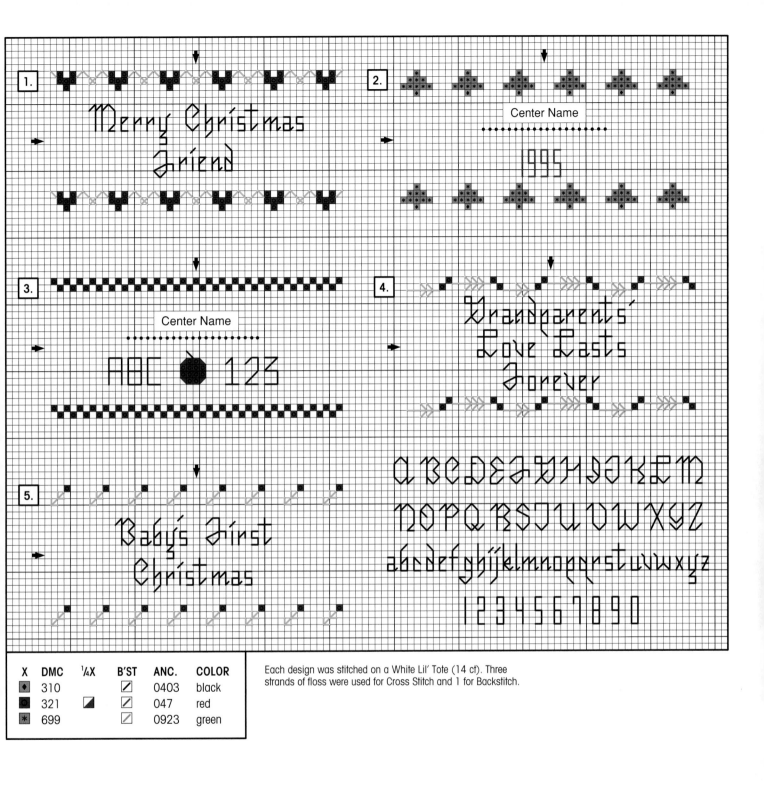

| X | DMC | ¼X | B'ST | ANC. | COLOR |
|---|-----|-----|------|------|-------|
| ◆ | 310 | | ╱ | 0403 | black |
| ◉ | 321 | ◢ | ╱ | 047 | red |
| ✳ | 699 | | ╱ | 0923 | green |

Each design was stitched on a White Lil' Tote (14 ct). Three strands of floss were used for Cross Stitch and 1 for Backstitch.

# HOLIDAY BASKETS

*These little baskets make cute holiday accents or gifts — and they're quick and inexpensive to make, too! We simply lined miniature market baskets with tiny cross-stitched cloths made by cutting standard bread cloths into quarters. For finishing touches, we adorned the baskets with ribbons and bows.*

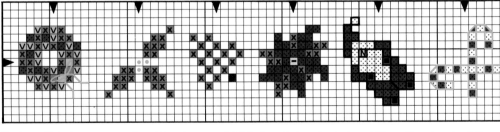

| MINI BREAD COVERS | | | | |
|---|---|---|---|---|
| **X** | **DMC** | **¼X** | **B'ST** | **JPC** | **COLOR** |
| ▨ | blanc | ⬝ | | 1001 | white |
| ■ | 300 | | | | brown |
| ■ | 310 | | ╱ | 8403 | black |
| ▦ | 321 | ◣ | ╱ | 3500 | red |
| X | 699 | | | 6228 | green |
| V | 701 | | | 6226 | lt green |
| − | 726 | | | 2294 | gold |
| N | 758 | | | 2331 | peach |
| ▨ | 321 | | | red Lazy Daisy |
| ⊙ | 321 | | | red French Knot |

Designs stitched on corners of mini bread covers, 4 fabric threads from beginning of fringe. Two strands of floss used for Cross Stitch and 1 for all other stitches.

For four mini bread covers, fold one Ivory Soft Touch™ (14 ct) Bread Cover in half with edges matched; cut along fold. Fold each half of bread cover in half with short edges matched; cut along fold. To complete fringe of each mini bread cover, ravel 8 fabric threads from cut edges of mini bread cover.

Using 1 strand of red or green floss, refer to photo to work Running Stitch (over and under 2 fabric threads) around sides of bread cover 2 fabric threads from beginning of fringe.

# Sweet Gesture

*For a sweet way to spread Yuletide cheer, top a jar of our Peppermint-Apple Jam with this Christmasy lid. Delivered in a doorknob basket, it's a holiday gesture everyone on your gift list will love.*

The design was stitched on a 6" square of Victorian Christmas Green Hardanger (22 ct). One strand of floss was used for all stitches. It was inserted in a small mouth jar lid.

For jar lid, use **outer edge** of jar lid for pattern and draw a circle on an adhesive mounting board. Cutting slightly inside drawn line, cut out circle. Using **opening** of jar lid for pattern, cut a circle of batting. Center batting on adhesive board and press in place. Center stitched piece on batting and press edges onto adhesive board; trim edges close to board. Glue board inside jar lid (**Note:** A mason jar puff up kit may also be used to finish jar lid.)

*Designed by Lorraine Birmingham.*

**43w x 34h**

| X | DMC | ¼X | B'ST | JPC | COLOR |
|---|-----|----|----|-----|-------|
| ▦ | blanc | ▢ | | 1001 | white |
| C | 309 | ◪ | | 3284 | lt red |
| | 310 | | ◿ | 8403 | black |
| ✳ | 321 | | | 3500 | red |
| O | 725 | ▢ | | 2298 | lt gold |
| ☆ | 782 | ◪ | | 5308 | dk gold |
| ▨ | 783 | ◪ | | 5307 | gold |
| ▲ | 816 | ◤ | | 3410 | dk red |
| V | 986 | | | 6021 | dk green |
| S | 987 | | | 6258 | green |
| ▢ | 988 | ▢ | | 6258 | lt green |

## PEPPERMINT-APPLE JAM

1½  pounds Granny Smith apples, peeled, cored, and coarsely chopped
1¼  cups water
¼  cup lemon juice
1  box (1¾ ounces) powdered fruit pectin
3  cups granulated sugar
1  teaspoon peppermint flavoring
   Red food coloring

Follow manufacturer's instructions to prepare canning jars, lids, and bands. In a food processor, process apples until finely chopped. In a Dutch oven, combine apples and next 3 ingredients over medium heat. Stirring constantly, bring to a rolling boil. Add sugar; stirring constantly, bring to a boil again and boil 1 minute longer. Remove from heat; skim off foam. Stir in peppermint flavoring; tint with food coloring. Pour jam into sterilized jars to within ¼-inch of tops. Wipe jar rims and threads; quickly cover with lids and screw bands on tightly. Invert jars 5 minutes; turn upright. Store in refrigerator or use water-bath method as recommended by the USDA to store at room temperature. When jars have cooled, check seals; refrigerate all unsealed jars.
**Yield:** about 2 pints jam

# Yuletide Trims

*These gleeful designs are sure to bring smiles! To add a bit of fun to the holidays, we stitched the miniatures on a bread cloth, a towel, a jar lid, and bag clips. You can spread even more Yuletide cheer by stitching these cuties on sweatshirts and afghans, too!*

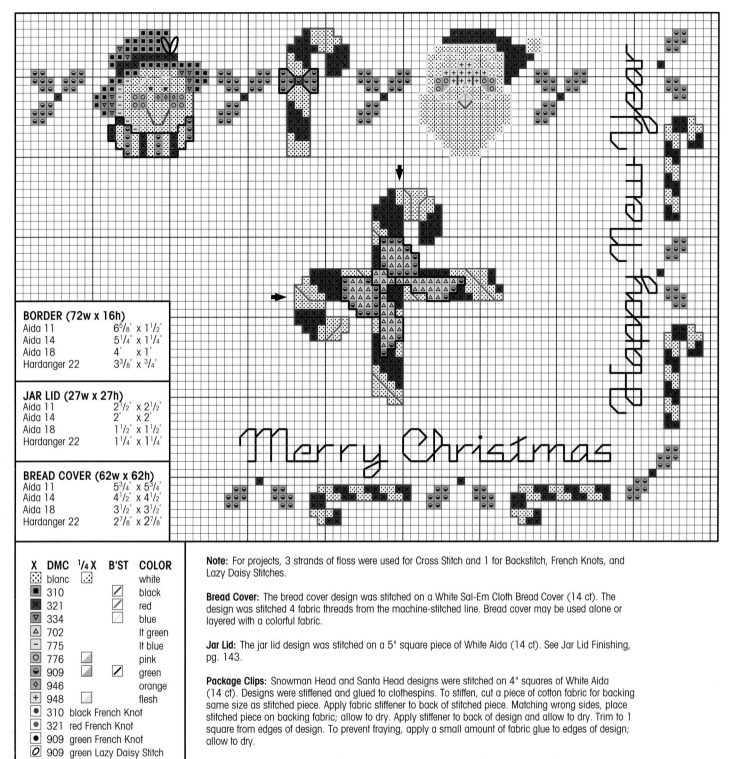

**BORDER (72w x 16h)**

| Aida 11 | 6⅝" x 1½" |
|---|---|
| Aida 14 | 5¼" x 1¼" |
| Aida 18 | 4" x 1" |
| Hardanger 22 | 3⅜" x ¾" |

**JAR LID (27w x 27h)**

| Aida 11 | 2½" x 2½" |
|---|---|
| Aida 14 | 2" x 2" |
| Aida 18 | 1½" x 1½" |
| Hardanger 22 | 1¼" x 1¼" |

**BREAD COVER (62w x 62h)**

| Aida 11 | 5¾" x 5¾" |
|---|---|
| Aida 14 | 4½" x 4½" |
| Aida 18 | 3½" x 3½" |
| Hardanger 22 | 2⅞" x 2⅞" |

| X | DMC | ¼ X | B'ST | COLOR |
|---|---|---|---|---|
| ▨ | blanc | ▨ | | white |
| ■ | 310 | | ╱ | black |
| ✕ | 321 | | ╱ | red |
| ▽ | 334 | | ╱ | blue |
| △ | 702 | | | lt green |
| − | 775 | | | lt blue |
| ◎ | 776 | ◪ | | pink |
| ◉ | 909 | ◪ | ╱ | green |
| ◇ | 946 | | | orange |
| + | 948 | ◪ | | flesh |
| ● | 310 | black French Knot | | |
| ● | 321 | red French Knot | | |
| ● | 909 | green French Knot | | |
| ⦰ | 909 | green Lazy Daisy Stitch | | |

**Note:** For projects, 3 strands of floss were used for Cross Stitch and 1 for Backstitch, French Knots, and Lazy Daisy Stitches.

**Bread Cover:** The bread cover design was stitched on a White Sal-Em Cloth Bread Cover (14 ct). The design was stitched 4 fabric threads from the machine-stitched line. Bread cover may be used alone or layered with a colorful fabric.

**Jar Lid:** The jar lid design was stitched on a 5" square piece of White Aida (14 ct). See Jar Lid Finishing, pg. 143.

**Package Clips:** Snowman Head and Santa Head designs were stitched on 4" squares of White Aida (14 ct). Designs were stiffened and glued to clothespins. To stiffen, cut a piece of cotton fabric for backing same size as stitched piece. Apply fabric stiffener to back of stitched piece. Matching wrong sides, place stitched piece on backing fabric; allow to dry. Apply stiffener to back of design and allow to dry. Trim to 1 square from edges of design. To prevent fraying, apply a small amount of fabric glue to edges of design; allow to dry.

**Towel:** The border design was stitched on the 14 count insert of a White Park Avenue Fingertip™ towel.

*Designed by Terrie Lee Steinmeyer.*

# Deck the Baskets

*Lined with any one of these holiday bread cloths, a basket of homemade Christmas goodies will be doubly appreciated! The sweet designs work up quickly, and they'll add a whole new dimension to your gift-giving.*

| X | DMC | ¼X | B'ST | ANC. | COLOR |
|---|------|-----|------|------|-------|
| | blanc | | | 2 | white |
| | 310 | | | 403 | black |
| | 320 | | | 215 | green |
| | 347 | | | 1025 | red |
| | 353 | | | 6 | peach |
| | 413 | | | 401 | dk grey |
| | 434 | | | 310 | brown |
| | 501 | | | 878 | dk green |
| | 676 | | | 891 | lt gold |
| | 677 | | | 886 | vy lt gold |
| | 722 | | | 323 | orange |
| | 729 | | | 890 | gold |
| | 743 | | | 302 | dk yellow |
| | 744 | | | 301 | yellow |
| | 799 | | | 136 | blue |
| | 800 | | | 144 | lt blue |
| | 815 | | | 43 | dk red |
| | 898 | | | 360 | dk brown |
| | 948 | | | 1011 | flesh |
| | 3072 | | | 847 | grey |
| | 3328 | | | 1024 | salmon |
| | 310 | | | 403 | black Fr. Knot |
| | 898 | | | 360 | dk brown Fr. Knot |

Grey area indicates beginning of fringe.

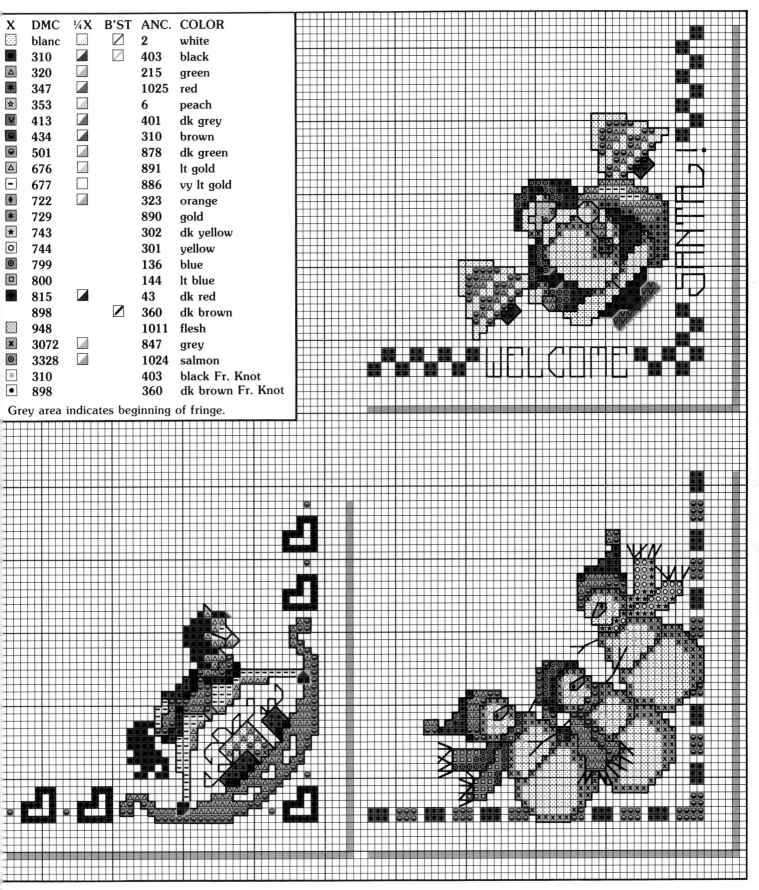

Each design was stitched on an Ivory Soft Touch™ Bread Cover (14 ct). Three strands of floss were used for Cross Stitch and 1 for Backstitch and French Knots.

*Designed by Deborah Lambein.*

# Little Drummer Bear

*Cheerfully playing a merry march, this little drummer knows Christmas music adds its own magic to the season. Stitched on a trio of holiday projects, he's a cute way to say "Merry Christmas."*

**Mug:** The design was centered and stitched on a 10 1/4" x 3 1/2" piece of Vinyl-Weave™ (14 ct) with bottom edge of design 8 squares from bottom edge of Vinyl-Weave™. Three strands of floss were used for Cross Stitch and 1 for Backstitch. Border design was continued to edges of Vinyl-Weave™. It was inserted in a Stitch-A-Mug™. Hand wash mug to protect stitchery.

**Towel:** The design was stitched on the Ivory Aida (14 ct) insert of a prefinished towel. Three strands of floss were used for Cross Stitch and 1 for Backstitch. Border design was continued to ends of insert.

**Mini Pillow:** Bear and Drum **only** were stitched on a 4 1/2" square of Ivory Aida (14 ct). Three strands of floss were used for Cross Stitch and 1 for Backstitch. Refer to page 18 for finishing instructions.

*Designed by Ann Townsend.*

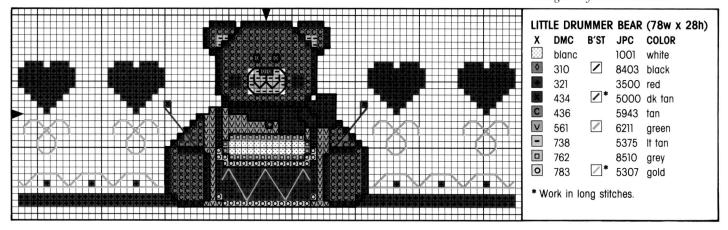

| X | DMC | B'ST | JPC | COLOR |
|---|---|---|---|---|
| | blanc | | 1001 | white |
| ◇ | 310 | ✓ | 8403 | black |
| ✚ | 321 | | 3500 | red |
| ✹ | 434 | ✓* | 5000 | dk tan |
| C | 436 | | 5943 | tan |
| V | 561 | ✓ | 6211 | green |
| − | 738 | | 5375 | lt tan |
| □ | 762 | | 8510 | grey |
| O | 783 | ✓* | 5307 | gold |

**LITTLE DRUMMER BEAR (78w x 28h)**

\* Work in long stitches.

# Easy Toppers and Tags

*This holiday season, top off a present of store-bought candy, homemade jam, or other goodies with one of these jar lid and gift tag sets stitched on perforated paper. Quick and easy to create, the designs are great beginner projects.*

**Note:** For all projects, see Using Perforated Paper, page 142.

**Jar Lids:** Designs #1 and #2 were each stitched on a 6" square of Natural Perforated Paper (14 ct). Three strands of floss were used for Cross Stitch and 1 for Backstitch. Design #1 was inserted in a small mouth jar lid; Design #2 was inserted in a large mouth jar lid.

For each jar lid, center jar ring over stitched design and draw a circle on perforated paper around **outside** edge of ring. Cut out stitched design, cutting slightly inside drawn line. Cut a piece of heavy bond paper the same size as stitched piece for backing. Glue stitched design inside jar lid; glue backing to wrong side of stitched piece.

**Gift Tags:** Designs #3 and #4 were each stitched on a 5" square of Natural Perforated Paper (14 ct). Three strands of floss were used for Cross Stitch and 1 for Backstitch. For Design #4, center design vertically with left edge of design 1" from one edge of paper; refer to photo and use alphabet provided to personalize tag.

For each gift tag, trim perforated paper 2 squares from edge of design on all sides. Cut a piece of heavy bond paper slightly larger than stitched design. Center and glue wrong side of stitched design to bond paper. Use a small hole punch to make a hole in bond paper for ribbon.

*Designed by Jane Chandler.*

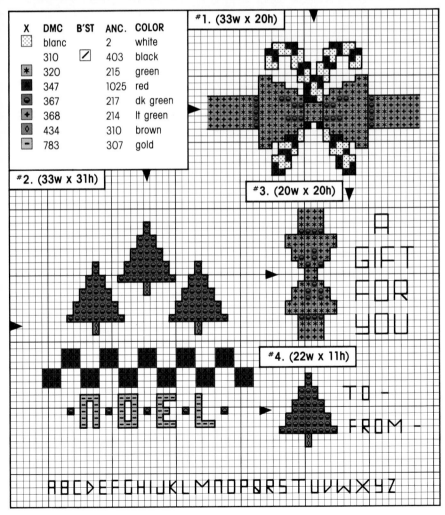

| X | DMC | B'ST | ANC. | COLOR |
|---|-----|------|------|-------|
| ▒ | blanc | | 2 | white |
| | 310 | ✓ | 403 | black |
| ✳ | 320 | | 215 | green |
| ■ | 347 | | 1025 | red |
| ◉ | 367 | | 217 | dk green |
| ✦ | 368 | | 214 | lt green |
| ◇ | 434 | | 310 | brown |
| – | 783 | | 307 | gold |

#1. (33w x 20h)

#2. (33w x 31h)

#3. (20w x 20h)

#4. (22w x 11h)

A GIFT FOR YOU

TO –
FROM –

ABCDEFGHIJKLMNOPQRSTUVWXYZ

# Merry Christmas Mugs

*Your favorite holiday drinks will be even more refreshing when you serve them in our cheery mugs! Stitched in bright red and green, the mugs can also be filled with candy to make quick little gifts or festive party favors.*

**Border Repeat**

**Border Repeat**

**Border Repeat**

| X | DMC | B'ST | ANC. | COLOR |
|---|-----|------|------|-------|
| ■ | 310 | / | 403 | black |
| ▨ | 666 | | 46 | red |
| ★ | 699 | | 923 | green |

Each design was stitched on a 10¼" x 3½" piece of Vinyl-Weave ™ (14 ct). Three strands of floss used for Cross Stitch and 1 for Backstitch. Center design on Vinyl-Weave™; extend borders to short edges. Inserted in a Stitch-A-Mug™. Hand wash mug to protect stitchery.

*Designs by Deborah Lambein.*

# Winter Warmer Gifts

*Gifts from your kitchen will be especially memorable when presented with any of these heartwarming projects for Christmas. The wintry wonderland motifs bring a cozy touch to mugs, jar lids, and lots more.*

**Jar Lids:** Tree Heart and Deer Heart from Hearts Border stitched separately on 6" squares of Fiddlers Lite (14 ct). Three strands of floss used for Cross Stitch. Inserted in small mouth jar lids. See Jar Lid Finishing, page 143. Decorate as desired.

**Mugs:** Cabin With Deer and Hearts Border stitched separately on 10½" x 3½" pieces of Vinyl-Weave™ (14 ct). Three strands of floss used for Cross Stitch. Inserted in Stitch-A-Mugs™.

**Towel:** Hearts stitched on Aida (14 ct) insert of an Ecru Velour Fingertips™ Towel. Four strands of floss used for Cross Stitch.

*Designed by Polly Carbonari.*

**Bread Cover:** Deer Heart, Snowflake Heart, and Bear Heart from Hearts Border stitched on a Deep Teal Royal Classic Bread Cover (14 ct) 4 fabric threads from beginning of fringe. Four strands of floss used for Cross Stitch. Cut a 3" square out of each corner. Machine stitch ½" from raw edges; clip inner corners diagonally to machine-stitched lines. Fringe fabric to machine-stitched lines.

**Gift Tag:** Cabin from Cabin With Deer stitched on a 6" square of White perforated paper (14 ct). Three strands of floss used for Cross Stitch. Trim to within 1 square of design.

| X | | DMC |
|---|---|---|
| + | | ecru |
| ■ | | 321 |
| ▮ | | 334 |
| ✳ | | 433 |
| C | | 436 |
| ✿ | | 561 |
| ◆ | | 562 |
| ◑ | | 725 |
| ☐ | | 3731 |

120w x 37h

71w x 25h

39w x 39h

137

# Reindeer Cheer

*Lined with our coordinating bread cloth, a basket of these deliciously spicy reindeer-shaped cookies will make a heartwarming holiday gift for friends or neighbors.*

## SPICY REINDEER COOKIES

- 1/3 cup butter or margarine, softened
- 1/3 cup vegetable shortening
- 1 3/4 cups granulated sugar
- 1 cup sour cream
- 2 eggs
- 1 teaspoon vanilla extract
- 5 1/4 cups all-purpose flour
- 1/4 cup cocoa
- 2 teaspoons baking powder
- 1 teaspoon baking soda
- 1 teaspoon salt
- 1 tablespoon ground cinnamon
- 2 teaspoons ground ginger
- 1 teaspoon ground allspice
- 1 1/4 cups sifted confectioners sugar
- 2 tablespoons milk

In a large bowl, cream butter, shortening, and granulated sugar until fluffy. Add sour cream, eggs, and vanilla; beat until smooth. In another large bowl, combine flour, cocoa, baking powder, baking soda, and salt; stir in spices. Add half of dry ingredients to creamed mixture; stir until a soft dough forms. Stir remaining dry ingredients, 1 cup at a time, into dough; use hands if necessary to mix well. Divide dough in half. Wrap in plastic wrap and chill 2 hours or until dough is firm.

Preheat oven to 350 degrees. On a lightly floured surface, use a floured rolling pin to roll out half of dough to slightly less than 1/4-inch thickness. Use a 2 1/2 x 3-inch reindeer-shaped cookie cutter to cut out cookies. Transfer to a greased baking sheet. Bake 7 to 9 minutes or until firm to touch. Repeat with remaining dough. Transfer cookies to a wire rack to cool.

In a small bowl, combine confectioners sugar and milk; stir until smooth. Spoon icing into a pastry bag fitted with a small round tip. Outline cookies with icing. Allow icing to harden. Store in an airtight container.

**Yield:** about 4 dozen cookies

| X | DMC | B'ST | ANC. | COLOR |
|---|---|---|---|---|
| ▨ | 310 | ✓ | 403 | black |
| ✚ | 320 | | 215 | green |
| ◉ | 347 | | 1025 | red |
| | 898 | ✓ | 360 | brown |

The design was stitched in one corner of an Oatmeal Sal-Em Cloth (14 ct) Breadcover, 6 squares from beginning of fringe. Three strands of floss were used for Cross Stitch and 1 for Backstitch.

*Design by Deborah Lambein.*

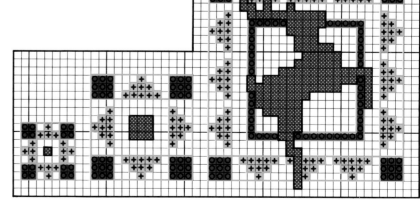

# Gingerbread Christmas

*This design gave us lots of cute ideas for holiday trimmings! Stitched on a mini pillow, the entire design adorns a decorative basket. The jelly jar motif is perfect when finished as a jar-lid topper, and the bread motif becomes a sweet gift tag. We also stitched a pair of the gingerbread men to dress up a bow.*

**HOME-COOKED CHRISTMAS**
**(67w x 39h)**

| X | DMC | B'ST | ANC. | COLOR |
|---|---|---|---|---|
| ▓ | blanc | | 02 | white |
| ◼ | 434 | | 0310 | brown |
| 6 | 435 | | 0365 | dk tan |
| V | 437 | | 0362 | tan |
| S | 563 | | 0204 | green |
| O | 680 | | 0901 | dk gold |
| − | 729 | | 0890 | gold |
| △ | 761 | | 08 | pink |
| | 844 | ◢ | 0401 | grey |
| ▢ | 3041 | | 0871 | violet |
| ✳ | 3328 | | 011 | dk pink |
| • | 844 | grey French Knot |

**ote:** For projects, 2 strands of floss were used for Cross Stitch, 1 for Backstitch, and for French Knot.

**asket: Home-cooked Christmas** was stitched on a 9" x 7" piece of Ivory Aida 14 ct). It was made into a mini pillow. Refer to page 18 for finishing instructions.

**ar Lid:** The jelly jar was stitched on a 5" square of perforated paper (14 ct). It was serted in a small mouth jar lid.

**Gift Tag:** The loaf of bread was stitched on a 5" square of perforated paper (14 ct) with the border 1 space from design on all sides. The right side of loaf was stitched to match left.

**Package Ornaments:** The gingerbread man was stitched on two 4" squares of perforated paper (see Using Perforated Paper, page 142). Trim to 1 square from edges of design.

*Designed by Polly Carbonari.*

# Christmasy Collection

*With these simple designs, it only takes a few stitches to create a little keepsake to accompany your Christmas food gifts. You can mix and match the motifs to create your own unique project, or you can use our design ideas. Either way, your holiday presentation will be a big hit!*

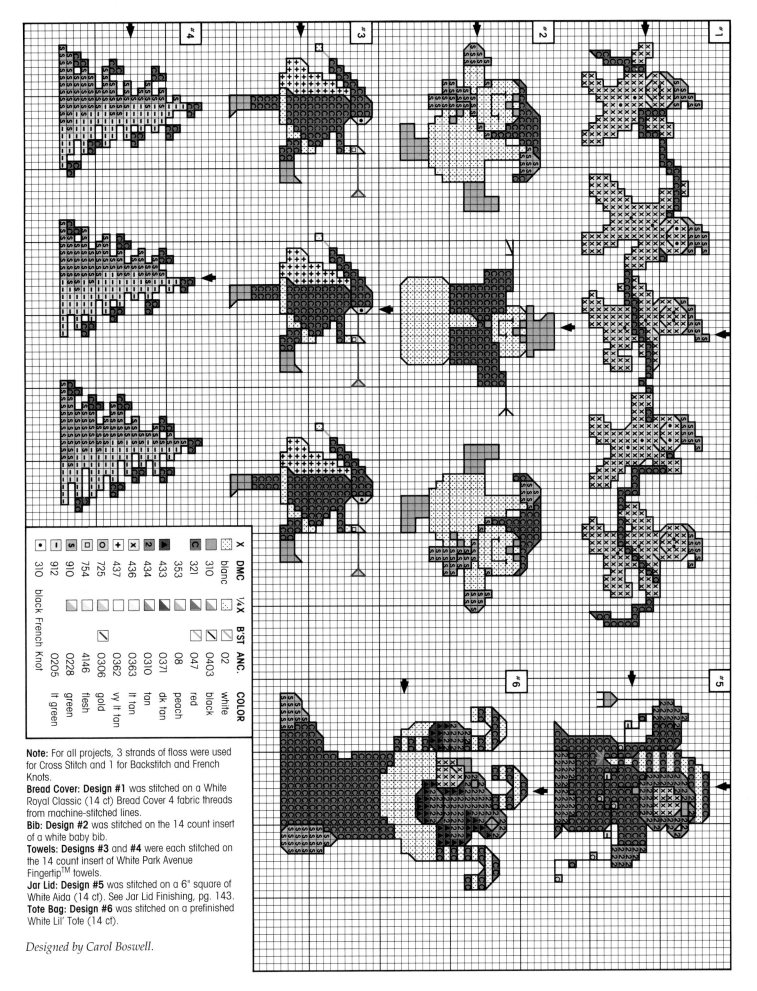

**Note:** For all projects, 3 strands of floss were used for Cross Stitch and 1 for Backstitch and French Knots.

**Bread Cover:** Design #1 was stitched on a White Royal Classic (14 ct) Bread Cover 4 fabric threads from machine-stitched lines.

**Bib:** Design #2 was stitched on the 14 count insert of a white baby bib.

**Towels:** Designs #3 and #4 were each stitched on the 14 count insert of White Park Avenue Fingertip™ towels.

**Jar Lid:** Design #5 was stitched on a 6" square of White Aida (14 ct). See Jar Lid Finishing, pg. 143.

**Tote Bag:** Design #6 was stitched on a prefinished White Lil' Tote (14 ct).

*Designed by Carol Boswell.*

# GENERAL INSTRUCTIONS
## WORKING WITH CHARTS

**How To Read Charts:** Each of the designs is shown in chart form. Each colored square on the chart represents one Cross Stitch. Each colored triangle on the chart represents one One-Quarter Stitch or one Three-Quarter Stitch. Black or colored dots represent French Knots. Black or colored ovals represent Lazy Daisy Stitches. The straight lines on the chart indicate Backstitch. When a French Knot, Lazy Daisy Stitch, or Backstitch covers a square, the symbol is omitted.

Each chart is accompanied by a color key. This key indicates the color of floss to use for each stitch on the chart. The headings on the color key are for Cross Stitch (**X**), DMC color number (**DMC**), One-Quarter Stitch (**¼X**), Three-Quarter Stitch (**¾X**), Backstitch (**B'ST**), J. & P. Coats color number (**JPC**) or ANCHOR (**ANC**), and color name (**COLOR**). Color key columns should be read vertically and horizontally to determine type of stitch and floss color.

**How To Determine Finished Size:** The finished size of your design will depend on the thread count per inch of the fabric being used. To determine the finished size of the design on different fabrics, divide the number of squares (stitches) in the width of the charted design by the thread count of the fabric. For example, a charted design with a width of 80 squares worked on 14 count Aida will yield a design 5¾" wide. Repeat for the number of squares (stitches) in the height of the charted design. (**Note:** To work over two fabric threads, divide the number of squares by one-half the thread count.) Then add the amount of background you want plus a generous amount for finishing.

## STITCH DIAGRAMS

**Counted Cross Stitch (X):** Work a Cross Stitch to correspond to each colored square on the chart. For horizontal rows, work stitches in two journeys (**Fig. 1**). For vertical rows, complete each stitch as shown (**Fig. 2**). When working over two fabric threads, work Cross Stitch as shown in **Fig. 3**. When the chart shows a Backstitch crossing a colored square (**Fig. 4**), a Cross Stitch should be worked first; then the Backstitch (**Fig. 7**) should be worked on top of the Cross Stitch.

**Fig. 1**

**Fig. 2**

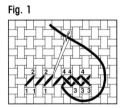

**Fig. 3**

**Fig. 4**

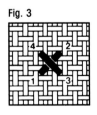

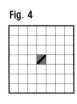

**Quarter Stitch (¼X and ¾X):** Quarter Stitches are denoted by triangular shapes of color on the chart and on the color key. For the One-Quarter Stitch (**¼X**), come up at 1 (**Fig. 5**); then split fabric thread to go down at 2. When stitches 1-4 are worked in the same color, the resulting stitch is called a Three-Quarter Stitch (**¾X**). **Fig. 6** shows the technique for Quarter Stitches when working over 2 fabric threads.

**Fig. 5**     **Fig. 6**

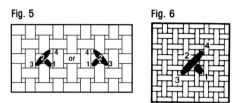

**Backstitch (B'ST):** For outline detail, Backstitch (shown on chart and on color key by black or colored straight lines) should be worked after the design has been completed (**Fig. 7**).

**Fig. 7**

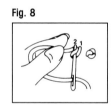

**French Knot:** Bring needle up at 1. Wrap floss once around needle and insert needle at 2, holding end of floss with non-stitching fingers (**Fig. 8**). Tighten knot; then pull needle through fabric, holding floss until it must be released. For larger knot, use more strands; wrap only once.

**Fig. 8**

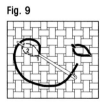

**Lazy Daisy Stitch:** Bring needle up at 1 and make a loop. Go down at 1 and come up at 2, keeping floss below point of needle (**Fig. 9**). Pull needle through and go down at 2 to anchor loop, completing stitch. (**Note:** To support stitches, it may be helpful to go down in edge of next fabric thread when anchoring loop.)

**Fig. 9**

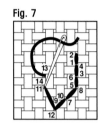

**Running Stitch:** Work Running Stitch as shown in **Fig. 10** stitching over and under desired number of fabric threads.

**Fig. 10**

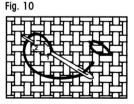

# STITCHING TIPS

**Working Over Two Fabric Threads:** Use the sewing method instead of the stab method when working over two fabric threads. To use the sewing method, keep your stitching hand on the right side of the fabric (instead of stabbing the fabric with the needle and taking your stitching hand to the back of the fabric to pick up the needle). With the sewing method, you take the needle down and up with one stroke instead of two. To add support to stitches, it is important that the first Cross Stitch is placed on the fabric with stitch 1-2 beginning and ending where a vertical fabric thread crosses over a horizontal fabric thread (**Fig. 11**). When the first stitch is in the correct position, the entire design will be placed properly, with vertical fabric threads supporting each stitch.

**Fig. 11**

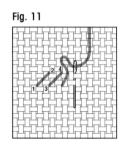

**Using Perforated Paper:** (**Note:** Perforated paper has a right side and a wrong side. The right side is smoother and stitching should be done on this side.) Do not fold paper to locate center. Use a ruler to measure width and height of paper; then mark lightly with a pencil at center of measurements. Perforated paper will tear if handled roughly; therefore, hold paper flat while stitching and do not use a hoop. Use the stab method when stitching; thread pulled too tightly may tear the paper. Carry floss across back as little as possible to prevent threads on wrong side of paper from showing through holes. After stitching, carefully erase visible pencil marks.

**Working on Waste Canvas:** Waste canvas is a special canvas that provides an evenweave grid for placing stitches on fabric. After the design is worked over the canvas, the canvas threads are removed, leaving the design on the fabric. The canvas is available in several mesh sizes.
1. Cut canvas 2" larger than design. Cover edges of canvas with masking tape. Cut a piece of lightweight, non-fusible interfacing the same size as canvas to provide a firm stitching base.
2. Find desired stitching area on clothing item and mark center of area with a pin.
3. Match center of canvas to pin on clothing item. With canvas threads straight, pin canvas to item; pin interfacing to wrong side. Baste all three thicknesses together as shown in **Fig. 12**.
4. Using a sharp needle, work each design, stitching from large holes to large holes.
5. Trim canvas to within ¾" of design. Dampen canvas until it becomes limp. Pull out canvas threads one at a time using tweezers (**Fig. 13**).
6. Trim interfacing close to design.

**Fig. 12**     **Fig. 13**

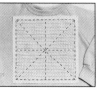

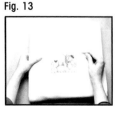

# FINISHING TECHNIQUES

## AFGHAN FINISHING

Cut off selvages. Fabric should measure 45"w x 58"h. For fringe, measure 5½" from raw edge of fabric and pull out one fabric thread. Beginning at raw edge of fabric, unravel fabric up to missing fabric thread. Repeat for each side. Using overhand knots, begin by tying a knot at each corner with four horizontal and four vertical fabric threads (**Fig. 14**). Working from the corners, use eight fabric threads for each knot until all threads are knotted.

**Fig. 14**

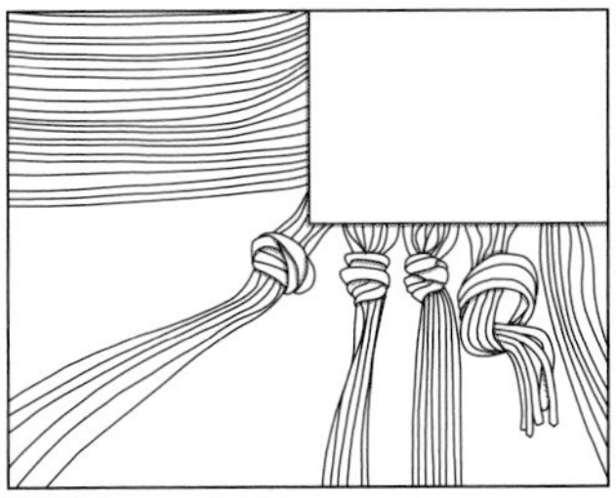

## BASKET TRIM FINISHING

To pad stitched piece, cut mounting board desired shape. Using board as a guide, cut a paper pattern ¾" larger than board. Centering pattern on design, cut out stitched piece. Clip ¼" into edges of stitched piece at ½" intervals. Cut batting same size as board; place on board. Place stitched piece on batting. smoothly fold and glue edges to back of board.

Cut prefinished cording the outer dimension of the board plus 1". Pin cording to back of board along outer edge. Opening ends of cording, cut cord to fit exactly. Insert one end of cording in the other; turn top end under ½". Glue cording to back of board along outer edge. Glue board to basket front.

## HEART ORNAMENT FINISHING

For each heart ornament, you will need tracing paper, an 8" square of Ivory Aida (14 ct) for backing, 10" x 5" piece of adhesive board, 10" x 5" piece of batting, 13" length of ¼" dia. cording with attached seam allowance, 2¼" tassel, six-strand embroidery floss for twisted cord hanger, and clear-drying craft glue.

For each heart pattern, fold tracing paper in half and place fold on dashed line of pattern; trace. Cut out traced pattern; unfold. Draw around small heart pattern, page 144, twice on adhesive board and twice on batting; cut out. Remove paper from adhesive board and stick one batting piece on each adhesive board piece. Center large heart pattern, page 144, over stitched piece; draw around pattern. Cut out stitched piece. Cut backing fabric same size as stitched piece.

For ornament front, clip ⅜" into edges of stitched piece at ½" intervals. Center stitched piece over batting side of one adhesive board piece; fold edges to wrong side and glue in place. Repeat with backing fabric and remaining adhesive board piece for ornament back.

Refer to photo for placement and glue cording seam allowance to wrong side of ornament front beginning at top point of heart. Glue tassel to wrong side of ornament front at bottom of heart.

For twisted cord hanger, cut two 30" lengths of six-strand embroidery floss (we used DMC 311, 500, and 902). Fold floss lengths in half and knot all ends together. Holding knot with one hand, insert one finger of other hand through loop of floss and twist until tight on finger. Holding floss so that it will not untwist, remove finger. Fold floss in half, matching the knot to the loop; knot them together. Holding knot with one hand, use other hand to stretch and slowly release

floss to make a smooth cord. Glue ends of cord to wrong side of ornament front at top of heart. Glue wrong sides of ornament front and back together. Weight with a heavy book until glue is dry.

## JAR LID FINISHING

Mason jar puff-up kits may be purchased for both regular and wide mouth jar lids; mounting instructions are included in kit. If a kit is not available, a padded mounting board can be made. Using flat piece of lid for pattern, cut a circle from adhesive mounting board. Using opening of screw ring for pattern, cut a circle of batting. Center batting on adhesive side of board; press into place. Center stitched piece on board and press edges onto adhesive. Trim edges close to board. Glue board inside screw ring.

## MINI PILLOW FINISHING

Cut a piece of Aida the same size as stitched piece for backing. With wrong sides facing, cross stitch fabric pieces together two squares from bottom and side design edges, making a cross stitch in every other square. Stuff with polyester fiberfill. Repeat to cross stitch across top of mini pillow two squares from design edge. Trim fabric ¼" from cross-stitched lines. Fringe fabric to one square from cross-stitched lines.

To make each twisted cord hanger, cut two 30" lengths of six-strand embroidery floss (DMC 319 was used for green; DMC 498 for red). Fold floss in half and knot all ends together. Holding knot with one hand, insert one finger of other hand through loop of floss and twist until tight on finger. Holding floss so that it will not untwist, remove finger. Fold floss in half, matching the knot to the loop; knot together. Holding knot with one hand, use other hand to stretch and slowly release floss to make a smooth cord. Whipstitch each end of cord to back of pillow at top corners.

## MINI WREATH FINISHING

For each mini wreath, refer to photo to wrap ¹⁄₁₆"w ribbon around a 3" dia. grapevine wreath; tie ribbon in a bow to secure. With design centered, cut stitched piece approx. 2¾" dia. Cut a piece of cardboard same size as stitched piece. Glue wrong side of stitched piece to cardboard. Glue right side of stitched piece to back of wreath. For ornament hanger, cut a 7" length of ¹⁄₁₆"w ribbon and fold in half; glue ends to top center of cardboard. Allow glue to dry.

## ORNAMENT FINISHING

For each ornament, cut stitched piece 1" larger than design on all sides. Use a piece of same fabric as stitched piece for backing; cut fabric the same size as stitched piece. With wrong sides facing, machine stitch fabric pieces together ½" from sides and bottom edge. Stuff with polyester fiberfill; machine stitch across top of pillow ½" from edges. Fringe fabric to one square from machine-stitched lines. Whipstitch ribbon to pillow for hanger.

## STOCKING FINISHING

**Note:** Please read instructions before beginning project.

1. Matching registration marks (★) and overlapping pattern pieces, trace stocking pattern (page 144) onto tracing paper and cut out.
2. Center pattern on wrong side of one 12" x 20" piece of stocking fabric and use a fabric marking pencil or pen to draw around pattern. DO NOT CUT OUT SHAPE.
3. Place stocking fabric pieces right sides together. Leaving top edge open, carefully sew stocking pieces together directly on drawn line.
4. Leaving a ¼" seam allowance, cut out shape. Clip seam allowance at curves and corners.
5. Cut a piece of interfacing slighter smaller than stitched piece. Follow manufacturer's instructions to fuse interfacing to wrong side of stitched piece.
6. For cuff, match right sides and short edges and fold stitched piece in half. Using a ½" seam allowance, sew short ends together to form a tube. Press seam open and turn right side out.
7. Repeat Steps 5 and 6 with cuff lining fabric. Do not turn cuff lining right side out.
8. For cording, lay cord along center on wrong side of bias strip. Matching long edges, fold strip over cord. Use zipper foot and machine baste along length of strip close to cord. Trim seam allowance to ½" and cut cording in half.
9. Matching right sides and raw edges and starting 1" from end of one cording piece, use zipper foot to baste cording to bottom edge of stitched piece. Open ends of cording and cut cord to fit exactly. Insert one end of cording fabric in the other; fold raw edge of top fabric ½" to wrong side and baste in place.
10. Place cuff lining and stitched piece right sides together. Using zipper foot and stitching as close as possible to cording, sew lining and stitched piece together along bottom edge. With wrong sides together and matching raw edges, fold cuff in half so that cording shows at lower edge; press.
11. Refer to Step 9 to baste cording to top edge of cuff.
12. Place cuff over stocking with right side of cuff facing wrong side of stocking and matching raw edges. With center of stitched design at center front of stocking, pin cuff in place. Using zipper foot, sew raw edges together close to cording. Turn stocking right side out. Fold cuff down over stocking.
13. For stocking lining, repeat Steps 2-4 using lining fabric pieces. Turn stocking lining right side out. Press top edge of lining ½" to wrong side. With wrong sides facing, insert lining into stocking.
14. For hanger, press long edges of fabric piece ½" to wrong side. With wrong sides together, fold hanger piece in half lengthwise; sew close to folded edges. Fold hanger in half to form a loop. Place ends of hanger between lining and stocking at heel side with approximately 1½" of loop extending above stocking; pin in place.
15. Slipstitch lining to stocking and, at the same, securely sew hanger in place.

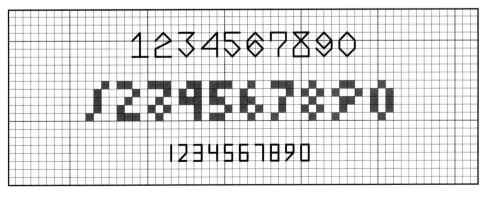

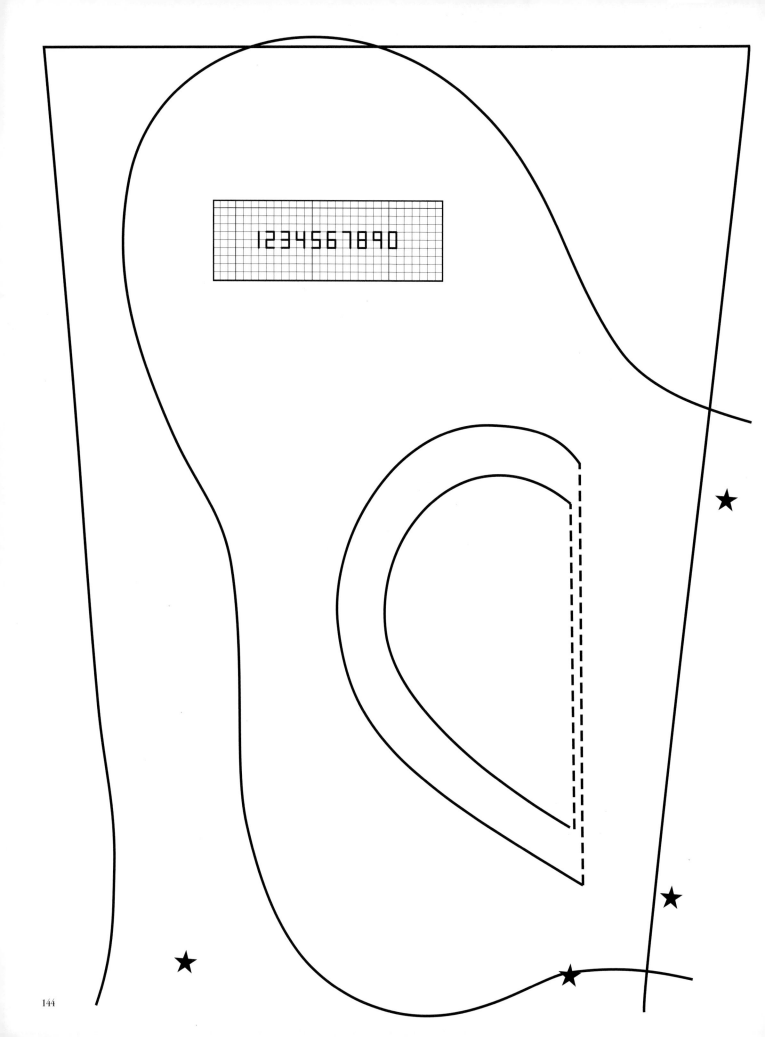

1234567890